ZOOM IN ...
South Africa

Teachers' Book

Herausgegeben von:
Iris Faßbender und Colette Granvillano

Erarbeitet von:
Iris Faßbender und Ebrusu Grimm

Unter Mitarbeit von:
Monika M. Jäger

Schöningh

Muttersprachliche Betreuung: Michelle Ruth Kloppenburg

www.schoeningh-schulbuch.de
Schöningh Verlag, Jühenplatz 1–3, 33098 Paderborn

Druck A 5 4 3 2 1 / Jahr 2019 18 17 16 15
Alle Drucke der Serie A sind im Unterricht parallel verwendbar.
Die letzte Zahl bezeichnet das Jahr dieses Druckes.

Umschlaggestaltung: Reinhild Kassing, Kassel
Umschlagabbildung: © Florian Kopp
Druck und Bindung: westermann druck GmbH, Braunschweig

ISBN 978-3-14-040657-4

Zur Arbeit mit dem Lehrerhandbuch

- Zur einfacheren Orientierung werden die Aufgaben wiederholt und in der Randspalte die entsprechenden Seitenzahlen des Schülerbandes angegeben.
- Zu jeder Aufgabe ist ein Erwartungshorizont formuliert, bei individuellen Schülerantworten ggf. eine Richtungsvorgabe.
- Weiterführende Unterrichtsideen zu den Aufgaben oder Vorschläge zur Unterrichtsgestaltung sind kursiv gesetzt. Über die Netcodes (s. unten) gelangt man zu den in den Vorschlägen vorgestellten Links.
- Zu jedem Kapitel findet sich ein zusätzlicher Text mit Aufgabenapparat und antizipierten Lösungen.
- Die Kopiervorlagen mit Hörverstehensaufgaben finden sich in den jeweiligen Kapiteln, wie auch die antizipierten Lösungen und die Transkripte der Texte.
- Ausformulierte Musterlösungen für alle drei Anforderungsbereiche sind als Kopiervorlage in den entsprechenden Kapiteln enthalten.

Webcodes

Webcodes verweisen auf Zusatzmaterial im Internet und erleichtern Ihnen das Auffinden von Links und Dateien, die speziell für den vorliegenden Band ausgewählt oder erstellt wurden.

@ SNG-40657-001

Zur Nutzung gehen Sie bitte auf folgende Seite: http://www.schoeningh-schulbuch.de/webcodes

Geben Sie dort den Code ein, um zu dem jeweiligen Material zu gelangen.

Contents

Getting started

SB p. 7

Describe the campaign poster and the photograph. Then draw the connection between both visuals, focusing on how both are dedicated to illustrating the impact of apartheid on South Africa's past and present.

Poster:

- A black child's head is placed on a citrus squeezer by a white hand, which seems to belong to someone who wears a black suit and a white shirt. Furthermore, the hand is inscribed with "APARTHEID" and the child's face of suffering can be seen. The poster's title is: NON AUX ORANGES OUTSPAN D'AFRIQUE DU SUD.
- The campaign poster is taking up the Blood-Citrus Topos: in the 1970s a consumer boycott was initiated against oranges (Outspan = Apfelsinen) by the anti-apartheid organization *Boycott Outspan Action* (BOA) which consisted of a small group of people from the Netherlands.
- Background information: the head in the images is a photograph of a boy playing among other children and his face was originally an expression of joy.
- Now the head serves as a symbol of excruciating pain administered by the collared hand of apartheid. The hand is not squeezing oranges but does what a hand does when squeezing a fresh orange.
  ➔ Impact: So, the cruel image on the poster wants to create a feeling of guilt whenever a European is consuming or especially squeezing an Outspan citrus fruit. The oranges with the fleshy interior serve as a metaphor for the human blood and flesh of the labourer. Furthermore, the squeezing of the head can be associated with the dissection of black South Africans.

Photograph:

- The photograph presents the seven pillars at the entrance to the Apartheid Museum in Johannesburg, depicting the fundamental values of South Africa's Constitution after apartheid.
  ➔ Impact: Thus, the architecture of the entrance symbolizes the architecture of the new constitution and of a new South Africa.

Both visuals are illustrating the impact of apartheid. The pillars stress the inherent human rights of South Africa's present in a positive and outsized manner. However, the poster, which was produced and published during apartheid in the 1970s, is using a more dreadful image to convince consumers to boycott South African products and, of course, to create awareness for the atrocities in South Africa's past.

Terra Nullius?
South Africa under Foreign Rule

M1 The Colonisation of South Africa

SB p. 8

1. Before reading, brainstorm in class: What do you already know about the colonisation of South Africa? Have a look at the pictures and their captions only to get some ideas.

With the help of the pictures and the captions, students should be able to recognize that South Africa was a country subject to colonisation by the Dutch and by the British (cf. painting of Riebeeck, map), that it obviously came to conflicts between the two of them (cf. caption below photograph on p. 10 showing the concentration camps), that it is very likely that there were also clashes between the settlers/colonisers and the native/colonised peoples (cf. map showing the remaining native states, statue of Shaka pointing at his importance), and that from 1910 on, the wind seemed to have shifted in British favour (cf. flag of South Africa from 1910 to 1928, with the British Union Jack in the top left-hand corner dominating the flag, in comparison with the crest representing the former colonies).

2. Make a timeline for the colonisation of South Africa. In doing so, use different lines and colours for native peoples, the Dutch settlers and the British ones. Show clearly where the lines either "collide" or "cooperate". Label the lines with important events.

KEY: *** native peoples —— Dutch settlers ----- British settlers

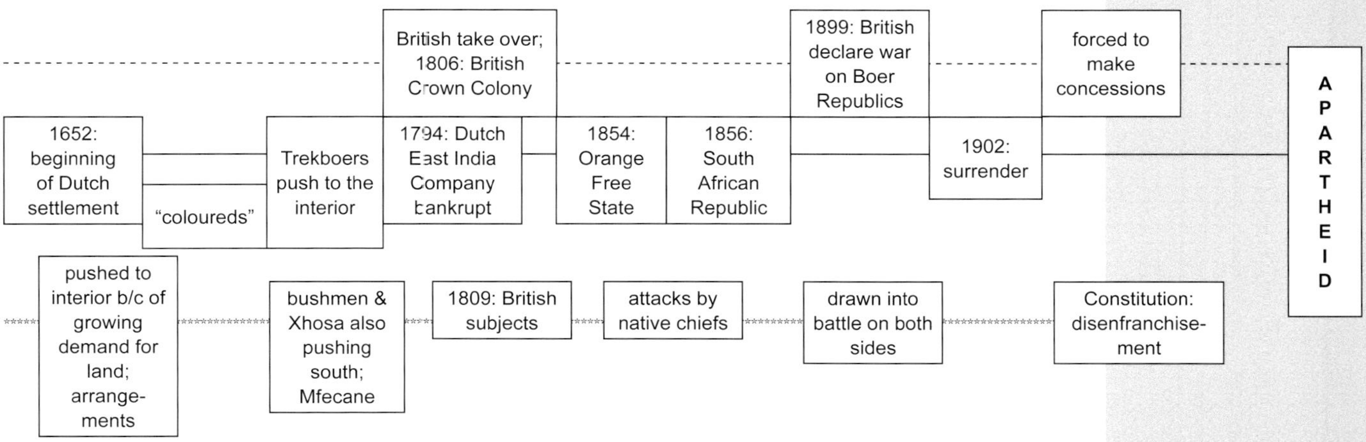

Collisions: Dutch settlers in the 17th century demanding more and more land and thus expelling natives from their land, forcing them to make arrangements; Trekboers pushing into the interior where they clash with bushmen and Xhosa people also pushing to the interior (but also: collisions between native peoples themselves due to Mfecane); British settlers forcing British citizenship on natives; attacks by native chiefs on British and Dutch colonies (republics); clashes between the Dutch and British colonies leading to the Anglo-Boer Wars; natives drawn into battle on both sides and thus also fighting each other; disenfranchisement of the natives, as embedded in the Constitution (asked for by the Boers, granted by the British)

Cooperation: mixing of races (e.g. "coloureds"); natives support troops in Anglo-Boer Wars (however: not voluntarily); forced British cooperation with the Boers after the end of the wars

3. **In the course of dealing with South Africa, you will frequently be confronted with issues in the past or today which can be traced back to South Africa's colonisation. Scan the text one more time for points in time which you believe had an impact on the further development of South Africa, or which are still important for South Africa today. Write them down on index cards.**

Individual answer; possible ideas:

SETTLERS' SEIZURE OF NATIVE LANDS	FORCED LABOUR & (ECONOMIC) EXPLOITATION OF NATIVE PEOPLES	CLASHES BETWEEN SETTLERS OF DUTCH AND OF BRITISH DESCENT
DISENFRANCHISEMENT OF THE NATIVE PEOPLES	...	...

M2 Confessions of Faith

Cecil Rhodes

SB p. 11

1. **Have a look at the quotation taken from the text. Paraphrase what exactly Rhodes suggests here, and why. Based on your results, hypothesize why Rhodes wrote this down privately and did not include it in his public appearances.**

Paraphrasis: Rhodes suggests the creation of a secret society which aims at promoting the interests of the British Empire and extending the sphere of its influence, such as uniting all English-speaking people under British rule and gaining back the lost American colonies.

Hypothesis: individual answer; at the time of New Imperialism (*Hochimperialimus*, c. 1880–1914, the time the source dates back to) the demand to expand the (British) Empire would not have to be concealed since this desire was shared by the major powers of that time (cf. e.g. the so-called Scramble for Africa – *Wettlauf um Afrika* – taking place at the time during which the African continent was basically divided like a cake between the powers; cf. ll. 21 ff.). However, especially the wish to "recover" the American colonies, lost after the American Revolutionary Wars, would certainly not have met with approval – especially on the side of the USA which, by the time Rhodes wrote, had completed its westward expansion "from sea to shining sea" and was a major empire, too (even though rather an "informal" empire). Also, a "secret society" would not make much sense when written about in public, of course.

2. **Imagine Rhodes, on his deathbed, had decided to share his private views on the destiny of the English [...] with the public. Present his views on the English and their tasks and justifications.**

The English are ...	That is why they should ... because ...
– ... unparalleled in the world as far as their exquisiteness and fine quality are concerned. – ... endowed with more honour and humanness than everyone else.	– ... expand their rule and settlements, if possible all over the world ... the human race will profit from it/the uncivilized will be better off/there will be more work/ultimately, it would mean world peace.

SB p. 12

3. **Examine how Rhodes emphasises his ideas by means of line of argument and choice of words.**

Line of argument: **ll. 1–2:** introduction – central question raised: how to be useful to one's country
ll. 3–14: answer to the question: why the English are destined to rule the world, how they should do this and which benefits await the world when the British rule
ll. 15–19: means to achieve the end (secret society to establish British rule over the world)
ll. 20–24: call to action – Britain shall partake in the Scramble for Africa
→ Rhodes's line of argument is structured in a clear and logical way, leading from the central question raised in the beginning to proposals, justifications, the way to achieve it, and culminating in the call to action to seize territory in Africa.

Choice of words:
- First-person personal pronoun "I" since he intends to present his private views and convictions (cf. e.g. ll. 3, 7, etc.)
- First-person plural pronouns "we"/"our" to create group identity/to establish common ground/to show that THE British are all on the same page/to create a contrast to THEM (to the other races in the world that are to be subjugated) (cf. e.g. ll. 4, 6, 7, 14, etc.)
- Repetitions to put emphasis on what is most important to him/to stress the urgency and importance of his demands (e.g. "I contend", ll. 7, 11; "simply means", ll. 14, 23; "duty", ll. 21, 22; etc.)
- Superlatives to show the unmatched quality of the British (cf. ll. 7, 24) and to establish a stark contrast to the "uncivilized" people ("the most despicable specimens of human beings", l. 9)
- Use of positively connoted words only to describe the British and so to convey that they indeed are worthy and entitled to rule the world (cf. e.g. ll. 7, 24)
- Degradation of the peoples to be ruled over by dehumanizing them ("despicable specimen", l. 9) and denying them culture/civilization (cf. l. 17) and thus justifying the necessity of British conquests
- Hyperboles to show the ultimate objectives (e.g. "the end of all wars", l. 14)
- Imagery of the "will-of-the-wisp" (l. 15) to hint at the mystical element that gradually evolves into a "plan" (l. 16), underscoring Britain's destiny to pursue an imperialist policy
- Use of contrasts (e.g. the British v. the "others"), also to stress the need to partake in the Scramble for Africa due to territorial losses in Britain's past (cf. l. 20) and to suggest that his vision is not merely a dream, but can come true ("What a dream, but yet it is probable, it is possible.", l. 19; also note the gradation included from "probable" to "possible")

Note: Stylistic devices have mostly been excluded from the analysis of the choice of words. Students should also be made aware of the fact that Rhodes also makes use of alliterations (cf. e.g. ll. 7f., 10f.,), parallelisms (cf. e.g. ll. 19, 20f.) and enumerations (cf. e.g. l. 24) to stress his ideas.

4. **Analyse the attitude towards other countries and their populations that becomes apparent in the text.**

It becomes very apparent and obvious that Rhodes has a very negative view of other countries and their populations and that he denies them their own civilization or culture, respectively the right to self-determination (as he proposes the British should rule over them, in the best case over the whole world). Since he regards the British as "the finest race in the world" (l. 7), it logically follows that all other races must by necessity be inferior to the British. This derogatory view is further underlined by his dehumanizing other races by calling them "despicable specimens" (l. 9), as if observed by a biologist, who should appreciate the blessings of British rule he describes in the following (cf. ll. 10ff.), or "uncivilised" (l. 17).

An dieser Stelle bieten sich zwecks Einordnung und späterer Bewertung der Rhodes'schen Aussagen weitergehende Recherchen zum Thema Imperialismus, theoretische Begründungen und Motive/Rechtfertigungen an. Ein früher Imperialismuskritiker ist zum Beispiel John A. Hobson [www.econlib.org/library/YPDBooks/Hobson/hbsnImp.html], zu den Motiven des Imperialismus ist von Bedeutung, dass die Recherche den Zivilisierungs- und Missionierungsgedanken beinhaltet wie auch sozialdarwinistische Begründungszusammenhänge berücksichtigt. Passend wäre hier auch die Beschäftigung mit dem Gedicht „The White Man's Burden" von Rudyard Kipling (1899), in dem er die „Zivilisierung" der „Wilden" als die „Bürde des weißen Mannes" bezeichnet.
Der Rhodes'sche Imperialismus wird zum Beispiel auch als „mystical imperialism" bezeichnet. Nach der Recherche könnte diese Etikettierung dann kritisch reflektiert werden, zum Beispiel unter Einbeziehung von Begriffen wie „chauvinism/jingoism" („Hurrapatriotismus").

5. **In 1908, the German Emperor Wilhelm II gave an interview to the British newspaper *The Daily Telegraph* in which he called the English "mad, mad, mad as March hares". [...] Discuss in how far this description fits to Rhodes, judged from a contemporary and from today's perspective.**
Individual answer; students should consider the speech against its historical backdrop of New Imperialism and thus judge Rhodes more leniently from a contemporary than from today's perspective since he basically expresses a common contemporary justification of imperialism (so his nation's sense of mission based on the belief in one's superiority over others, especially the allegedly "uncivilized" peoples). However, even (British) contemporaries would probably have found his suggestion of forming a secret society with the expressed aim of regaining the United States awkward, to say the least.

Eine weitere diplomatische Krise zwischen Großbritannien und Deutschland löste Kaiser Wilhelm II durch das sogenannte „Krüger-Telegramm" (1896) aus, gesendet an den Buren-Präsidenten Paul Krüger (vgl. SB, S. 16), in dem er Krüger zur erfolgreichen Abwehr des Jameson Raid, eines Angriffs der britischen Truppen im Zuge der Burenkriege, gratulierte. Dies könnte an geeigneter Stelle mit in den Unterricht einfließen, zum Beispiel als Wiederholung von M 1 oder vorbereitend auf die Recherche zu Krüger (M 4), ggf. auch als Referatsthema.

SB p. 13

6. **Describe the cartoon. Check out the skills pages for tips and language support. Then write a speech bubble for Rhodes that contains the gist of Rhodes's statements made in M 2.**
Description:
The cartoon is dominated by the over-dimensional figure of a man who is standing on and towering over a piece of land. Both his legs and arms are stretched out, his feet, clad in boots, are standing on the northern and southern outer edges of the piece of land, his arms pointing in the same directions. The man is holding a helmet in his right hand, and a rifle is attached to his belt. Strings connect his feet to his hands, and his hand to his belt.
Speech bubble: Individual answer; British superiority and resulting duty to "seize" African territory should be included.

7. **Against the backdrop of your results from the tasks, evaluate the appropriateness of satirizing Rhodes as "The Rhodes Colossus".**
Individual answer; the cartoon satirizes Rhodes's megalomania of attempting to "paint the map red" (red spots symbolizing British-ruled territories) by means of a railroad and a telegraph line connecting Africa "from Cape to Cairo", i.e. from south to north, which was quite an enterprise at the given time, especially since the French colonisers were pushing from east to west (and were thus bound to clash with the British). In the text, megalomaniac aspects can similarly be seen, as for example in the vision of a world under British domination, or in the expressed objective of "recovering" the United States of America.

Um den Schülern die Idee Rhodes' zu veranschaulichen, bietet es sich an, ihnen eine Karte des „Wettlaufs um Afrika" zu zeigen (s. Webcode). Daraus wird schnell ersichtlich, dass es sich um ein im Grunde nicht realisierbares Projekt handelte.

SNG-40657-001 @

M3 Following the Equator

Mark Twain

SB p. 13

1. **Have a look at Twain's introduction to Chapter XVIII that is given in the speech bubble above. What does it reveal about a) Twain's view on the British and their Empire and b) the style of the text you are about to read? Briefly talk to a partner and makes notes on your expectations.**
Individual answer; the quotation is characterized by its quite obvious sarcasm since Twain purports the British to be mentioned in the Bible already. He refers to the British expansion ("the sun never set(s) on the British Empire"), having colonies all over the world. Thus he foreshadows that they will "inherit the earth". The sarcasm is also revealed because he specifically quotes a sentence that characterizes the ones who will "inherit the earth" as "meek" – a description unfit to talk about the British since the establishment of an Empire of such extent requires conquest and domination.

2. **Describe the "Rhodesian methods", according to Twain.**
Twain characterizes the "Rhodesian methods" as clinging to the ones used in former times, unlike the more modern and, according to Twain, humane ways of eradicating unwished for parts of the population, such as using poison. He describes Rhodes and his followers as robbers and slayers, pursuing their ways under the pretext of legality, by first pretending to want to buy the native lands and then to instigate trouble and take the land by force. Twain states that the native kings are deceived and killed and that their cattle are seized afterwards. He accuses Rhodes of forcing the native people into slavery and of not taking responsibility for the well-being of the people afterwards. All in all, Twain claims he would prefer the "modern" methods of being killed instead of a slow death lasting for many years under the "Rhodesian methods".

3. **Examine how Twain makes use of sarcasm to utter criticism on Cecil Rhodes and his way of dealing with the native peoples. Relate your findings to your ideas from task 1.**
Examples of sarcasm:
- Euphemisms, e.g.: "humanest way of *diminishing*" (l. 4); "the *reduction* of the population" (l. 17)/"humanely *reduce(d)* an *overplus* of ..." (ll. 19/20/21); "*right-hearted* Australian pioneer" (ll. 20 f.)
- Open sarcasm, e.g.: "all must go except ... terms to be decided by himself" (ll. 1–3) → arbitrariness of white rule; double standards; "Mr. Rhodes and his gang" (l. 5) → criminals; "the hallowed old style of 'purchase' for a song" (l. 8) → revealing traditional way of deception & trickery under the pretext of benefiting the robbed

and conquered peoples; "All these are admirable and worthy of praise" (ll. 22 f.) ➔ revealed as sarcasm since Twain speaks about killing people in the "modern" way, e. g. by using poison; "I admire him ... buy a piece of the rope for a keepsake" (ll. 28 f.) ➔ Rhodes will be killed for his doings, and rightly so

- Use of punctuation/quotation marks to reveal deceit and deception used by Rhodes (cf. ll. 8, 11, 19)
- Drastic comparison of the "old" and "modern" ways of killing "undesired" parts of the population, respectively the comparison between the native peoples and dogs to stress the absurdity and cruelty of Rhodes's proceedings (cf. ll. 19 ff.)

Task 1: Students should on the one hand identify sarcasm as characteristic of Twain's writings here, and should on the other hand link the biblical quotation to the "Rhodesian methods" which turns the quotation more or less upside down since these methods can hardly be ascribed to somebody who is meek at heart.

SB p. 14

4. Compare the way Twain describes Rhodes with Rhodes's utterances in M 2.

Even though the way Rhodes's self-perception and Twain's outside view of him might seem conflictive at first glance, a connection can nevertheless be established between the two texts. Taking into consideration the way Rhodes sees the British, namely as superior and destined to rule the world, and how he sees other peoples, namely as inferior and destined to be ruled over by the British, it follows that the British would have the right to treat the natives the way that Twain describes as the "Rhodesian methods" in his travelogue, for example taking their land and property away.

5. Assess the accuracy of Twain's remarks, taking into account Twain's American background as well as the immediacy of his observations.

Individual answer; students should consider that the immediacy of Twain's observations might actually speak for their accuracy (since he was on the spot and also had the opportunity to observe British rule elsewhere in the Empire during his travels), but that his American background might bias his views on British rule (the USA as former colonies of the British, the Declaration of Independence, the USA's "manifest destiny" to be the "nation of futurity" [Sullivan] since they were a nation born unaffected by the fetters of a monarchical past and destined to bring democracy to the world).

6. In 2004, Cecil Rhodes was voted 56th in a South African TV series on "Great South Africans" (top 100). Against the backdrop of M 2 and M 3, write a letter to the person in charge at the TV channel in which you comment on this choice.

Individual answer; results from M 2 (self-perception and plans/objectives, including the "Rhodes Colossus" cartoon) and M 3 (heavy criticism levelled against Rhodes's methods of exploitation from an outside, American view) should find consideration; the letter should be a formal one ("Sir or Madam" ... formal style ... no complimentary close, but name and place of residence of writer only), the writer should introduce him-/herself and give reasons for writing the letter, the comment should be a balanced assessment, a conclusion on the issue in question should be drawn from the argumentation.

7. Draw a cartoon that shows Cecil Rhodes from Twain's perspective.

Individual answer; based on the text, it would make sense to draw Rhodes as a criminal, for example as a pirate (cf. l. 26), as a slave-holder with a whip (cf. ll. 12 ff.) or as a robber (cf. ll. 9 f., 26).

Weiterführend/vertiefend bietet sich eine Recherche/eine Präsentation zur „American Anti-Imperialist League" an, die sich im Jahr 1898 formierte, um gegen die Annexion der Philippinen im Zuge des Spanisch-Amerikanischen Krieges zu protestieren und deren Mitglied Twain wurde, nachdem er anfangs den Spanisch-Amerikanischen Krieg enthusiastisch unterstützt hatte. Motive für seinen Sinneswandel könnten also im Zentrum der Recherche/Präsentation stehen (Beispiel: s. Webcode).

@ SNG-40657-002

M4 Britain's Imperial Destiny

William Scawen Blunt

1. Scan M 1 once more for information about the time period the text is concerned with: What issues were the British confronted with in South Africa, and what do you expect Scawen Blunt's stance towards this to be, and why? Briefly talk to a partner and make some notes.

SB p. 15

Issues the British were confronted with:

- Resistance of Boer Republics against British attempt to unify and dominate them
- 1899: British declaration of war on Orange Free State and South African Republic (Transvaal)
- 1899–1902: Anglo-Boer Wars end with the defeat of the Boers, but the British nevertheless have to make concessions to the Boers

Scawen Blunt's probable stance:

Individual answer; it is to be expected, however, that students would rather believe him to sympathize with the British and that they would find their proceedings and claims justified and legitimate (since Scawen Blunt himself was British).

2. Give a summary of Scawen Blunt's writings on 15th June 1899 and point out his predictions for the British Empire he makes on 22nd and 31st January 1900.

15th June 1899:

Scawen Blunt describes Britain's plan to re-annex the Transvaal. This, according to Scawen Blunt, is to be done by means of an aggressive dispatch by the governor of Cape Colony, commissioned by the colonial secretary, meant to arouse public opinion and to instigate war between Britain and South Africa. This is also because former trickeries have been tried in vain because of the cleverness of Kruger. Scawen Blunt assumes the Empire sees the time as opportune due to Germany and France being distracted, and he further believes the Boers will fight back. This, he hopes, might help to improve the situation of the black South Africans. Finally, Scawen Blunt criticizes the British martial ways, especially since simultaneously general peace is mediated in The Hague.

22nd/31st January:

He predicts the disintegration and collapse of the British Empire due to its never-before-seen wickedness and its hypocrisy.

3. Analyse Scawen Blunt's attitude towards British imperialism, as it becomes apparent in the given diary extracts.

In general, Scawen Blunt holds a very negative view of British imperialism and the British Empire. This becomes apparent in various ways:

- He sees through the British scheme to instigate war, e.g. calling it a "plot" (l. 1), clearly naming the function ("to force the hand of the government", l. 2), characterizing its tone ("the most aggressive kind", ll. 3 f.), naming the impact a "chorus" (l. 5) – underlined by the alliteration of the newspapers being "full of flame and fury" (l. 4).
- He explains why Milner is excellent at war-mongering and has been chosen because of that by outlining the latter's former deeds (cf. ll. 6 ff.) and by characterizing him as "quite an extremist as an imperial agent" (l. 10) and thus as "invaluable to the empire builders" (l. 12).
- He clearly sympathizes and sides with the native peoples who are affected negatively by British rule (cf. ll. 19 ff.).
- He is looking forward to revealing the hypocrisy of the British imperialists who start a war while simultaneously general peace conditions are being negotiated at The Hague (cf. ll. 22 ff.).

- He clearly labels the imperialists as "thieves" (l. 27) to underscore the illegality of their doings and sarcastically calls their division of the booty "amicable" (l. 27).
- He exposes the moral double standards and hypocrisy of the British by juxtaposing their deeds and the support of the Queen and the politicians (cf. ll. 30 ff.).
- He predicts the self-inflicted disintegration and collapse of the British Empire (cf. ll. 30, 34 f.).

4. With the help of M 1, explain Scawen Blunt's references to the situation in South Africa.

Cf. task 1: Scawen Blunt writes about the preliminary events leading to the Anglo-Boer Wars from 1899 to 1902.

SB p. 16

5. Scawen Blunt mentions the Boer President of the Transvaal, Paul Kruger, in lines 14 and 17. Do further research on Oom (Uncle) Kruger, especially as far as his political ideas are concerned. Based on your findings, discuss if Paul Kruger is an appropriate choice to name one of South Africa's most famous national parks – Kruger National Park – after.

Individual answer; pros and cons should be considered (see below; more research on the Gold Rush and resulting economic and political measures implemented by Kruger in the Transvaal are recommended though).

Paul Krüger (Stephanus Johannes Paulus Krüger, 1825–1904) wurde als Sohn von Siedlern deutscher Herkunft in der britischen Cape Colony geboren und streng calvinistisch erzogen. Im Jahr 1852 wurde er Zeuge, wie der damalige Repräsentant des Transvaal, Andries Pretorius, einen Vertrag mit den Briten abschloss, der den Buren nördlich des Flusses Vaal die Unabhängigkeit garantierte, und von 1855 bis 1856 war Krüger Teil einer Kommission, die die Grenzen der neuen Republik Transvaal abstecken sollte. Als es in den Jahren von 1861 bis 1864 zu Unruhen kam, kämpfte er als Kommandant für die Einheit und Befriedung des Landes auf Basis einer verfassungsgemäßen Autorität.
Als die Briten im Jahr 1877 den Transvaal annektierten, kämpfte Krüger für die Unabhängigkeit der Region und reiste zweimal nach Großbritannien, wo er vergeblich versuchte, den britischen Premier Benjamin Disraeli von seiner Sache zu überzeugen, woraufhin er maßgeblich an der Organisation eines passiven Widerstands gegen die Briten beteiligt war. Als auch der neue Premier William Gladstone Krüger die Unterstützung verweigerte, gelang es ihm, die Cape Colony für den Widerstand zu mobilisieren und mit dem Transvaal zu einem Bund zu vereinigen. Nach militärischen Auseinandersetzungen mit den Briten gelang es Krüger, einen Frieden zu verhandeln, der eingeschränkte Unabhängigkeit garantierte. 1883 wurde Krüger zum Präsident des wiederhergestellten Transvaal gewählt. Dieses Amt behielt er bis zum Jahr 1902, in dem sich die Buren den Briten nach den Burenkriegen geschlagen geben mussten. Vor Ende der Burenkriege wanderte Krüger nach Holland aus, 1904 starb er in der Schweiz.
Krüger wird oft als der „Vater der Afrikaner-Nation" bezeichnet, womit aber dezidiert die Buren gemeint sind. Sein Leitspruch „Afrika den Afrikanern" lässt sich zurückführen auf den Goldrausch, mit dem der Transvaal Ende des 19. Jahrhunderts konfrontiert war und der dazu führte, dass mehr und mehr Ausländer auf der Suche nach Wohlstand einwanderten. In dieser Zeit wurden Krüger und Cecil Rhodes, als Vertreter der Cape Colony, zu Erzfeinden.
Krüger legte den Grundstein für die Errichtung des Kruger National Park, der seines Zeichens der berühmteste und größte des Landes ist. Nachdem im späten Jahrhundert einige Tierarten aufgrund von Jagd zu verschwinden begannen, propagierte Krüger die Idee von Nationalparks, in denen gefährdete Tierarten sich in ihrer natürlichen Umgebung ohne menschliche Einflussnahme fortpflanzen sollten.

M5 Ngoba ... sewuthi (Because ... you now say)

B. W. Vilakazi

1. Have a look at the imagery taken from the poem. Copy the table, writing down the image in one column, the denotation [...] in another column, and use the third column to write down your connotations [...]. Speculate on who is talking to whom here, and discuss what kind of relationship is represented in the poem.

SB p. 17

Image	Denotation	Connotation
"You then say that I am like a **pole**" (l. 7) → simile, personification	a long post usually made of wood or metal, set upright in the ground to support something	individual answer, e.g.: strong, resistant and insensitive to what is going on
"You say that I am like a **rock**." (l. 16) → simile, personification	a hard solid mineral substance	individual answer, e.g.: hard, durable and insensitive to harm or pain
"You say that I am an **animal**." (l. 26) → metaphor, personification	a living creature that is not a plant or a person	individual answer, e.g.: having only basic needs and instincts

From the images above the student may infer that the poem is about a master-slave relationship, with the slave ("I") making his master ("You") face the stereotypical ideas he has of the speaker's nature.
Note that, separated from the context of the poem, the first two images could also be interpreted as positive views on a person's strength and solidity.

2. Describe what the speaker of the poem (= a black person working in a mine) is doing and point out his interpretations of how his (white) employer will judge his actions.
The speaker, a black mine worker, explains to his white employer that there is a big difference between how the mine workers behave (external appearance) and what they actually think and feel (inner nature). The fact that they smile or sing and dance does not mean they are content with or insensitive to the painful working conditions in the mines. Even though they have not had an education and live in poor conditions, they are human beings deserving respect and love. The speaker wants to show his employer that the opinions he has formed are false and unjust.

3. Imagine the employer was Cecil Rhodes (cf. M 2). Turn the poem into a dialogue between the speaker of the poem and Rhodes as the owner of the diamond mine.
Individual answer; the following aspect should, however, find consideration: In this dialogue, Mr Rhodes, who was convinced of the supremacy of the British, is likely to emphasise the fact that his black employee should be grateful for having been given a job in his mine and that, if there should be the slightest doubt or sign of contradiction, he will be fired (cf. 3rd stanza, l. 27: "readily replaced").

4. Analyse the employer's attitude towards the speaker. Focus on the composition of the poem and how the poet makes use of imagery in a progressive way.
The poem is composed like a dialogue in the course of which the speaker wants to make his employer aware of the deplorable situation of black mine workers. Each of the four stanzas begins with "Because", a conjunction used when giving reasons for a statement made before. Thus, the addressee is shown why he has gained those wrong impressions. For the same purpose the poet uses strong imagery. Simile, metaphor and personification are arranged in a progressive way, from comparisons with inanimate objects in the first two stanzas ("pole", "rock") via a comparison with a low-living creature in the third stanza ("animal") to that with a physically and intel-

lectually handicapped person in the fourth ("deaf-mute ... simple dupe"). Alliteration (e.g. l. 14 "hand holding", l. 19 "let loose", l. 27 "readily replaced"), repetition, parallelism (e.g. ll. 1, 9, 18, 28, 32 "Because", ll. 3, 23 "Singing", "sing", ll. 8/9, 16/17, 26/27, 36 ff. "You ... say/think ... That ...) and the contrastive use of pronouns (e.g. "I, my, myself, me" = speaker v. "you" = addressee v. "we, our" = the speaker's "kind" v. "they" = white capitalists) additionally highlight the sharp contrast between the employer's attitude towards the speaker and his fellow workers and reality.

@ SNG-40657-003

Eine umfangreiche Analyse des Gedichts als Protest gegen soziale Ungleichheit findet sich unter dem nebenstehenden Webcode.

5. **Against the backdrop of the text, discuss how effective poetry as a form of protest can be.**
Individual answer; note that, in Zulu tradition, poetry is often accompanied by dance and music. Therefore, it is a popular means used to stimulate large audiences' interest and empathy and sometimes spur them into action.

SB p. 18

6. **Watch the performance of imbongi Albert Nyathi on *YouTube*. [...]**
Individual answer.

Bei dieser Performance handelt es sich um „Senzeni Na?“ (What Crime Have We Committed?), ein Anti-Apartheid-Lied, das Albert Nyathi am Todestag des Aktivisten Chris Hani geschrieben haben will und das gelegentlich mit dem amerikanischen Protestsong „We shall overcome“ verglichen wird. Im Internet kursieren zwei unterschiedliche Versionen des Refrains (s. u.):

What have we done?	What have we done, what have we done?
Our sin is that we are black?	What have we done, what have we done?
Our sin is the truth	What have we done, what have we done?
They are killing us	What have we done in this country (world)?
Let Africa return	Boers are dogs
	Boers are dogs
	Boers are dogs
	Boers are dogs
	It's a sin to be black
	It's a sin to be black
	It's a sin to be black
	It's a sin in this country (world)

http://en.wikipedia.org/wiki/Senzeni_Na%3F [01.08.2014]

@ SNG-40657-004

Im Internet findet sich auch ein Interview mit Nyathi, in dem er u. a. über Senzeni Na spricht.

M6 The National Flag of South Africa, 1928 – 1994

SB p. 19

1. **Describe the flag.**
The flag consists of three horizontal stripes which, from top to bottom, are coloured in orange, white and blue. In the centre of the white stripe, one can see three rather tiny flags, the one in the middle positioned vertically, the other two horizontally. The very left one has a blue background and is dominated by a red cross and with red line extending diagonally to the very corners of the flag. The one in the middle has vertical white and orange stripes and features a tiny square in its top left-hand corner, consisting of three more vertical stripes, coloured red, white and blue from left to right. The very right flag shows three horizontal bars coloured red, white and blue from top to bottom and one vertical green stripe on its very left side.

2. **Compare the flag with the national flag from 1910 to 1928 (cf. M 1).**
The major difference between the flags is that the older one features a Union Jack which is very dominant in the top left-hand corner of the flag, symbolizing British domination, and that the former colonies are merely subsumed in a crest. The "new" flag from 1928, in contrast, seems to have created something genuinely new by the focus on the "oranje – blanje – blou" and the incorporation of the three flags (Union Jack, flags of the Republic of the Orange Free State, and of the Transvaal) on the same level and in the same size in its centre.

3. **Explain in how far the new flag expresses a compromise between the South Africans of Boer and of British descent.**
The fact that the three flags in the centre are on the same level and in the same size shows that the South Africans of Dutch and of British descent are of equal importance and are equal in status.

4. **Have a look at the points in time that you have written down on index cards (cf. M 1, task 3). Have you written down anything that explains why a compromise seemed to have been necessary at all? If so, what did you write down? If not, check M 1 once more.**
In 1910, when the first national flag was designed, there was no need for a compromise as such because the British had reigned supreme in the Anglo-Boer Wars. However, M 1 already suggests that there was to be need for compromise in future, because the Boers were in a dominant position in South Africa, even though they had been defeated by the British. That is why the British had to make concessions to them back then.

In Vorbereitung auf das nächste Kapitel sollten die Schüler darauf hingewiesen werden, dass die einheimische Bevölkerung in der Gestaltung der Flagge offenbar keinerlei Berücksichtigung findet. An dieser Stelle könnte bereits das Wort Apartheid eingeführt werden, die Schüler könnten Definitionen selber schreiben und bereits Überlegungen anstellen, auf welche Lebensbereiche sich Apartheid beziehen könnte (vgl. Info-Box im SB, S. 20).

Land Claims Open Pandora's Box

Kwanele Sosibo

Kwanele Sosibo, a former rapper, studied journalism in Durban before joining the *Mail & Guardian* as a reporter.

South Africa has eleven 'kings' who are financed by the state (cf. graphic), but that number may soon increase as more and more traditional leaders are laying claim to precolonial land.

1. Before reading the text, do some research on the Restitution of Land Rights Amendment Act of August 2014. Prepare a five-minute talk and give it in class.

2. **Outline** the impact of President Zuma's call for traditional leaders to lodge land claims, as presented in this article.

3. Against the backdrop of your knowledge about Mfecane and King Shaka's wars of conquest, **explain** why King Goodwill Zwelithini insists on claiming Zulu land from 1838 onwards.

4. **Examine** Sosibo's attitude towards the latest land claims. Focus on the presentation of facts and his use of language.

5. Imagine you were one of Zulu King Goodwill Zwelithini's many children. Write an e-mail to the editor, **commenting** on Sosibo's article.

Land claims open Pandora's box*

President Jacob Zuma's call for traditional leaders to claim old land may do more harm than good.

The Bapo ba Mogale*, who this week signed a R546-million* share deal with Lonmin*, were one of a number of chieftaincies placed under administration by the North West province because of long-running disputes between rival branches of the ruling lineage.

With pressure mounting to push the deal through, and Lonmin desperate to meet its black economic empowerment requirements, the province hired an academic to determine the bona fides* of the members of the royal family who would form the core of the reconstituted council.

Gavin Capps, a senior researcher at the Mining and Rural Transformation in Southern Africa project at the University of Witwatersrand who has been observing the situation closely, notes that "these kind of genealogical disputes are the very stuff of political competition in Tswana* formations, and claims to familial rank are frequently manipulated to mobilise popular support or legitimate the victors".

"So what we are really seeing here is the use of a state-appointed ethnographer* to stabilise a tribal authority by cementing the claims of one faction over the others," he said. "This is exactly what used to happen under apartheid, but the difference today is that these interventions are increasingly connected with securing the conditions for mining corporations and determining who will benefit from their local operations."

Presidential encouragement

In February, at the opening of the National House of Traditional Leaders in Cape Town, President Jacob Zuma urged traditional leaders to "find good lawyers" and "look at the claims on behalf of your people, so that no one is left outside".

Historians and researchers working in the area of land rights and cultural studies have argued that his statements earlier this year at the opening of the National House of Traditional Leaders in Cape Town can be seen as helping chiefs entrench* their custodianship* of the land within their jurisdiction.

Capps says "the continued strengthening of the chieftaincy by the ANC* means some 17-million people living in the former homeland areas – a sizeable chunk* of the South African population – are increasingly confronted by a different form of political power than people in urban areas are, which defines them as subjects rather than citizens".

This year a flurry* of enormous land claims were publicly announced by several royal families, kicked off by the Zulu king, Goodwill Zwelithini ka-Bhekuzulu, whose Ingonyama Trust announced that it was planning to claim for land under the control of the Zulu kingdom in 1838.

In public, the Ingonyama Trust's chairperson, Jerome Ngewnya, has said the boundaries of the kingdom are still being researched.

Rock solid proof

The East Griqua, a Khoisan community in Kokstad, announced that its claim would be the biggest because rock art found all over the province proved that the Khoisan were the first people in the province.

The Hlubi people are also demanding restitution* and financial compensation for the same tract of land as the Zulu king. The Restitution of Land Rights Amendment Act*, recently signed into law, only refers to the reopening of land claims after the 1913 cut-off line.

Maanda Mulaudzi, a historian based at the University of Cape Town, says the question we should be asking as a society is: What is the point of kings and chiefs?

"We are a democracy; we shouldn't conflate* African culture with kings and chiefs. People can have a culture without having chiefs. I have no sympathy for the view that customs are unchanging. That's how they were ethnographed by colonialism. Dynamic African culture dictates that I can choose whether or not I want to be under a chief."

Kwanele Sosibo, "Land Claims Open Pandora's Box", Mail & Guardian, http://mg.co.za, 14.08.14 [06.01.2015]

to open Pandora's box to start sth. that will cause a lot of other problems
Bapo ba Mogale community in Bapong near Rustenburg
R546 million c. 38 million Euros
Lonmin British producer of metals operating in South Africa
to determine the bona fides to check that they are who they say they are

Tswana Bantu-speaking people

ethnographer scientist who studies and compares the different races of people

to entrench to establish forever
custodianship responsibility for taking care of sth.
ANC cf. SB p. 24
chunk a large amount

flurry a time when there is suddenly a lot of activity

restitution the act of giving back something that was stolen to its owner, or of paying for damage
Restitution of Land Rights Amendment Act (of August 2014) re-opens the lodgement period for restitution claims to allow people to put claims until June 30, 2019
to conflate to combine two or more things to form a single new thing

6. **Describe** the cartoon.

7. **Explain** its message.

8. **Discuss** whether the cartoon is an appropriate commentary on Sosibo's article.

1. **Before reading the text, do some research on the Restitution of Land Rights Amendment Act of August 2014. Prepare a five-minute talk and give it in class.**
Download of 2014 Amendment Act: see Webcode

SNG-40657-005 @

Example of **cue cards** structuring the five-minute talk:

Restitution of Land Rights Amendment Act (August 2014) passed by the National Assembly and National Council of Provinces, signed into law by President Jacob Zuma **offers a solution to people who lost their land as a result of racially discriminatory practices**		
What's new? **re-opens the lodgement period for restitution claims** **new deadline:** **June 30, 2019** (old deadline expired in 1998) **claims** prior to the 1998 deadline **shall be prioritised** BUT how to deal with deals lodged on the same land before and after 1998?	**1913 cut-off date** **traditional leaders intend to lodge claims from 1838 onwards** **prominent example:** King Goodwill Zwelithini claims the province of KwaZulu-Natal, taken from the **Zulu** **during the colonial period,** first by the Voortrekkers, then by the British	'heritage' policy under discussion according to a draft policy document by the government, **land shall be redistributed rather than restituted to people dispossessed pre-1913** specific pieces of **land shall be allocated as heritage sites and historical landmarks**

2. **Outline the impact of President Zuma's call for traditional leaders to lodge land claims, as presented in this article.**
The call may have fewer advantages than disadvantages (cf. sub-heading).
On the one hand, the government as well as companies operating in South Africa have to meet the Black Economic Empowerment (BEE) demands by giving certain disadvantaged groups economic privileges that were previously not available to them. On the other hand, the re-opening of land claims is a decision that will entail a rash of problems. Several traditional leaders have announced their intention to lodge restitution claims to vast and overlapping swaths of land back to precolonial times. The problem is that different groups occupied the same land at different times, as wars raged and people moved around. So, the chiefs or 'kings' laying claim to land presently owned by the state or non-black South Africans, will have to furnish solid proof of their community's land property rights and also of their own claim to the 'throne'. The role of state-appointed ethnographers in this process is seen rather critically in the text: partisan as they may be, the ethnographers could create benefits at will for certain chiefs or certain mining companies, an undemocratic behaviour pattern reminiscent of colonial times.

3. **Against the backdrop of your knowledge about Mfecane and King Shaka's wars of conquest, explain why King Goodwill Zwelithini insists on claiming Zulu land from 1838 onwards.**
Information about Zulu King Shaka, including a 50-minute video:
www.blackstarexodus.com/shaka-zulu.html (see also Webcode above)
Mfecane: a term used to describe the rise of the powerful Zulu King Shaka and his wars of conquest (cf. SB p. 9)
Map: the rise of the Zulu empire under Shaka in the first half of the 19th century

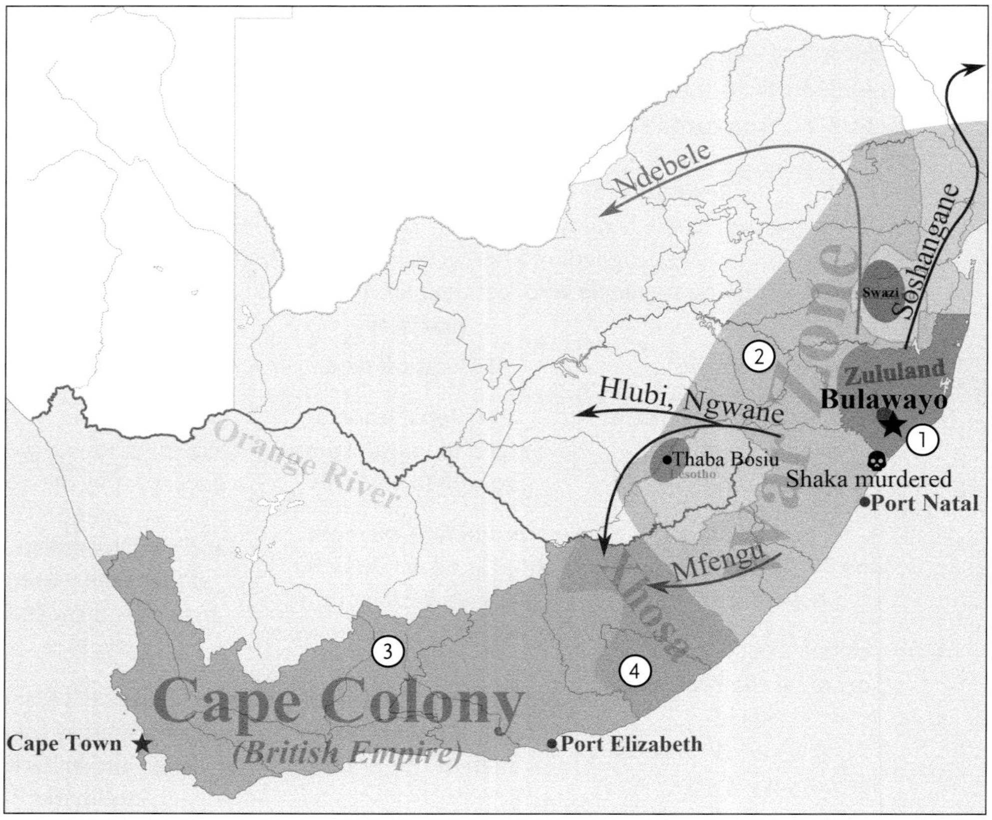

"Shaka's Empire map" by Discott – Own work, licensed under CC BY-SA 3.0 via Wikimedia Commons, http://commons.wikimedia.org [05.02.2015]

This map illustrates the rise of the Zulu Empire under Shaka (1816–1828) in present day South Africa. The rise of the Zulu Empire (1) under Shaka forced other chiefdoms and clans to flee across a wide area of southern Africa. Clans fleeing the Zulu war zone (2) included the Soshangane, Zwangendaba, Ndebele, Hlubi, Ngwane, and the Mfengu. A number of clans were caught between the Zulu Empire and advancing Voortrekkers and British Empire (3) such as the Xhosa (4).

The current consensus among historians is that the Zulu kingdom of the 19th century was bordered by the Thukela River in the south, the Pongola in the north, the Mzinyathi to the west and the Indian Ocean to the east.
Subsequently, King Goodwill Zwelithini insists on laying claim on Zululand from 1838 onwards.

4. Examine Sosibo's attitude towards the latest land claims. Focus on the presentation of facts and his use of language.
Right from the beginning, Sosibo's opinion is obvious: the heading and sub-heading leave no doubt that the journalist is not in favour of re-opening the lodgement period for restitution claims. The metaphor used in the heading, "Pandora's box", refers to severely detrimental and far-reaching consequences of the decision, the sub-heading ("may do more harm than good") confirms the reader's first impression, even though the use of the auxiliary "may" only indicates a possibility or probability, not yet an already determined future.
The overall impression of the article is matter-of-factly: news is presented on "this week's ... deal" (l. 4) or the latest claims of some communities (cf. ll. 40–44), for example. Looking a bit more closely at the language used in this news, you will, however, detect words that are negatively connoted, e.g. the deal was "push[ed] ... through" due to "pressure mounting" (l. 7), the company benefitting from the deal was "desperate" for success (l. 7), President Zuma is helping chiefs to "entrench" their custodianship (l. 27), etc.

Quoting reliable experts, mainly a senior researcher from the University of Witwatersrand (cf. ll. 11–20, 29–32) but also a historian from the University of Cape Town (ll. 46–51), Sosibo intends to make the reader trust him and eventually share his view. The choice of quotations speaks volumes: both researchers are highly critical of the new Amendment Act and its consequences. Capps criticises manipulations (cf. l. 14f.) and graphically speaks of "cementing the claims of one faction over the others" (l. 17). He warns of turning citizens living in the former homeland areas into mere subjects (cf. ll. 29–32), which would be unworthy of a democracy. Mulaudzi sings from the same hymn sheet when asking for the point of kings and chiefs today (cf. ll. 47–51).

5. **Imagine you were one of Zulu King Goodwill Zwelithini's many children. Write an e-mail to the editor, commenting on Sosibo's article.**
Individual answer; expected is an argumentation from a historical point of view, manifesting the future heir's claim to ancient Zululand.

6. **Describe the cartoon.**
In the centre of the cartoon, an old white farmer and an equally old black farmhand are having a break after work. It is early evening, and the two are standing in front of a fenced-in flock of sheep, smoking and looking relaxed.
In the background you can see the farmer's pick-up, a flat-topped hill and a wind-powered water pump hardly able to irrigate the vast, barren landscape.
The focus of attention lies on the large-size speech bubble above the two men. The farmer is asking his farmhand, named Petrus, which half of the farm's debts he would like to take over.

7. **Explain its message.**
The message the cartoonist is trying to convey is that owning farmland does not necessarily make you rich. South Africa's land is not always productive and profitable, like that in the cartoon, which shows the typical non-productive Karoo vegetation. The cartoonist does not tackle the need of restitution in principle; it is the mode of compensation that is questioned here. The farmer is deeply indebted and will not be able to repay the debts in his lifetime. His question of which half of the farm's debts Petrus is going to settle is a joke, indicating the cartoonist's conviction that the whole restitution of land rights policy is but a farce.

8. **Discuss whether the cartoon is an appropriate commentary on Sosibo's article.**
Individual answer; basically, the cartoonist and Sosibo, respectively the experts he quotes, are of the same opinion. The blog the cartoon has been taken from, however, is a right-wing one, attacking the so-called "left-wing hypocrisy" and allowing racists like "whiteson" to advance their discriminatory opinions.

Long Walk to Freedom

M1 Cry, the Beloved Country

Alan Paton

M1a Excerpt 1 (from chapter 9)

SB p. 21

1. **Describe the picture, then collect characteristics of townships that you know about in class [...].**
The picture shows a house being built of adobe with a corrugated-iron door. It was taken in 1948 in a township near Johannesburg. A black woman is sitting, a black man kneeling in front, seemingly preparing the next move with simple building supplies. The shantytown seems to be under construction or the couple's new home is located at the edge of the town.
In South Africa, townships are places that once were officially designated for black occupation by apartheid legislation. They are usually built on the periphery of towns and cities, mostly because people cannot afford living in those towns and cities. Township homes like the one in the picture are almost always built on land that is not owned by the occupier, so they are there illegally. Severe problems to cope with in townships are the lack of water, electricity and sewerage, among others.

2. **Describe the coming into being of the shantytown presented in the text and present what is going on in- and outside the newly-built "house".**
In the excerpt at hand, Orlando, a township in the urban area of Soweto, goes up overnight. The weather is warm and dry so that loads of makeshift homes are quickly built of iron, sacks and plank, and the few lucky ones among the new occupants have even been able to procure discarded chimney pipes for heating. The rent is one shilling a week, collected by Dubala, a powerful black politician, and his committee, who are responsible for the construction of Shanty Town, a project that draws attention from the press.
Outside the newly-built "house" mentioned in the text people are making a lot of noise: apart from construction noise there is plenty of polyglot singing, joking and laughing around a warming fire.
Inside the makeshift home the action focusses on a woman and her sick daughter. It is quiet, dark and cold but the girl burns with fever and dies before a doctor can attend to her. The mother had to move her child despite her illness because the date for the move to Orlando could not be postponed.

3. **Based on your results from tasks 1 and 2, explain if – or to what extent – the shantytown depicted in the picture could possibly be the one described by the narrator in the given excerpt. Give proof from the text to support your standpoint.**
Cf. model solution, worksheet 2.

4. **Analyse by which means the author makes this excerpt resemble a gospel sung in Church. Focus on language and stylistic devices.**
Like in a gospel, the prose of the novel excerpt is simple (short and concise sentences, connected by "and", if at all, e.g. ll. 4/5, 11, 19) and intermixed with religious intonations and references (cf. ll. 3 ff. "I shall ... and you my wife ... and you my son ...",

ll. 32 ff. "... there is a lovely valley ... The water sings ... the wind cools ...", ll. 34 f. "God ... Christ ... have mercy upon us", ll. 36 ff. "*Nkosi sikelel' iAfrika*"). The frequent use of conventional symbols such as light and darkness (ll. 1, 2, 11, 27) or warmth and cold (ll. 11, 26, 27, 30, 33) represents the dualistic view of the world prevalent in the Christian faith (heaven/hell, good/bad). Repetitive scraps of dialogue from anonymous speakers (ll. 3–7, 12–15) and more repeated phrases ("Shanty Town is up overnight", ll. 16, 22, 26, "Quietly my child", "your mother is by you", ll. 28, 29, 30/31, 32, 34) or the repetition of the negation in the final sentences, used for emphasis, underscore the impression that the text is spoken rhythmically. Reading the text aloud, you can imagine the gospel singers' frequent clapping to the beat of the lyrics. The didactic and emotional message, expressed at the end of the excerpt, is also gospel-like: the main solace comes from your faith in God, and if you believe strongly enough, you will be able to bear all kinds of hardships (here, for instance, the death of your child).

5. The narrator describes the singing of *Nkosi sikelel' iAfrika*, which can be translated as "Lord Bless Africa" (in Xhosa). [...] Taking into account that the author Alan Paton could take it for granted that his readership was familiar with the song and its meaning, explain in how far the inclusion of it in the scene described adds to emphasising the religious-like character of this excerpt. SB p. 22

Nkosi sikelel' iAfrika is a deeply religious pan-African liberation anthem that communicates the message of God's love and forgiveness. Exemplifying certain groups of the African society (men, women, youths, etc.) it intends to establish an inextricable bond between all humans praying to God and asking for his blessing. The anthem's message thus contributes to the Christian overtone of the given text excerpt.

Es empfiehlt sich, wenn möglich, den Schülern an dieser Stelle das Video von „Nkosi sikelel' iAfrika" (Lord Bless Africa), eine Hommage an Nelson Mandela, vorzustellen (siehe Webcode und auch M 10c, SB S. 46).

SNG-40657-006 @

Lord, bless Africa;
May her horn rise high up;
Hear Thou our prayers
And bless us.

Chorus:
Descend, O Spirit,
Descend, O Holy Spirit.

Bless our chiefs
May they remember their Creator.
Fear Him and revere Him,
That He may bless them.

Bless the public men,
Bless also the youth
That they may carry the land with patience
and that Thou mayst bless them.

Bless the wives
And also all young women;
Lift up all the young girls
And bless them.

Bless the ministers
of all the churches of this land;
Endue them with Thy Spirit
And bless them.

Bless agriculture and stock raising
Banish all famine and diseases;
Fill the land with good health
And bless it.

Bless our efforts
of union and self-uplift,
Of education and mutual understanding
And bless them.

Lord, bless Africa
Blot out all its wickedness
And its transgressions and sins,
And bless it.

www.endarkenment.com/kwanzaa/nkosi/versions.htm [14.01.2015]

M 1b Excerpt 2 (from chapter 12)

SB p. 22

1. The title of the novel is *Cry, the Beloved Country*. What does this title reveal about Patton's attitude towards South Africa and how he sees the current state of affairs? Briefly talk to a partner and exchange ideas.

The title, in the form of an imperative, asks for a social protest against the structures that would give rise to apartheid soon after the book was published. Paton adores his country but in order to restore its beauty and power he calls for strong-voiced complaint. The verb "cry" is here used in the sense of "require or suggest strongly a remedy or disposition". (www.merriam-webster.com/dictionary/cry [05.02.2015])

2. Summarise what the various parties presented in the text want and complain about, and point out the narrator's conclusion.

In this excerpt, the dichotomies in the South-African society are revealed: Blacks and whites demand different measures in matters of residency, labour, education and, consequently, opportunity. Many of the problems with South Africa such as the degrading of the land reserved for the natives, the disintegration of tribal community and the flight to the urban areas have led to racial segregation, inequality and social disorder. Disagreement is the only certainty when all of the African voices cry out what must be done.

Another prevalent theme is the detrimental effect of fear on the characters and society of South Africa. The narrator concludes that, due to the baleful circumstances described, fear grips the black and white population alike. Unborn children will inherit this fear and be unable to love and relish their country because the more they love it, the greater will be their pain.

3. Examine how the author underlines the vicious circle of inequality and injustice that has a detrimental effect on South Africa's society. Consider recurrent structures and contrasts.

The first half of the excerpt (cf. ll. 1–12) has a clearly distinct antithetical structure. By juxtaposing a number of different voices, some of which are sympathetic and some that are profoundly unsympathetic to the black Africans, Paton lays bare the stark differences of opinion that divide the white population. An emphatic "Yes" introduces the second part of the text (l. 13), followed by questions that are not rhetorical ones, for the author himself does not know the answers (cf. ll. 13–15, 18). In this part, antithesis continues (e.g. "one cries this thing, and one cries another"). In the last part (cf. ll. 20–24) Paton draws a conclusion, a thought that has already been introduced in lines 18 and 19, namely that of fear as the driving force behind all misery, present and future. Imperatives combined with constant repetition stress the importance of the author's judgement, which begins with the phrasing of the title "Cry, the beloved country" (l. 20).

Throughout the text, repetition is the dominant means of emphasis, either the repetition of key words such as "cry", which occurs eight times, or "fear" (ll. 18, 20, 24) or the repetition of phrases – anaphora and parallelism – such as "Who knows how ..." (ll. 14, 18) or "Let him not ..." (ll. 20–23).

To put it in a nutshell, the contrastive and repetitive structure of the text reflects its contents, the repeated futile attempts to make South Africa speak in one voice.

4. In German, the title is translated as "Denn sie sollen getröstet werden". Evaluate the appropriateness of this translation against the backdrop of your findings from M 1a and M 1b.

Individual answer; students should mention that the verb "cry" here resembles some kind of call to action, whereas the German title rather calls for consolation for the ones who suffer, but is not necessarily a direct call to action as such. Against the backdrop of the given excerpts, both titles would make sense if one interprets the situation of the black South Africans as a call to action to change something about their living conditions (they are forced to build up "shantytown" because of a lack of appropriate accommodation), but also as a reason why they should be consoled or given comfort.

5. **Have a look at the two film posters for the 1951 and the 1995 film versions of *Cry, the Beloved Country*. Describe both, also focusing on similarities and differences.** SB p. 23

Left poster: Film title quite dominant in the bottom right-hand corner; image of three people above title: (probably black) person holding a pointed pistol in his right hand, his face veiled except for the eyes; a woman with dark hair, and an elderly man with greyish-white hair and a moustache in the top right-hand corner. Left of the film title, one can see a man kneeling down and touching another person lying on the ground; above those two, there is a group of people illustrated, probably a family of native people due to their clothing and their different sizes, wandering to the East. Left of them, there is a tree bending in the wind that seems to be blowing heavily. In the top centre, setting apart the pictorial elements, one can read an advertising slogan for the film version of Paton's novel. Storm clouds are gathering in the background; it looks as if the landscape was burning.

Right poster: Film title in the very centre of the poster, presented in black letters against a yellow circle; the bottom part depicts a green and idyllic landscape, with a road leading towards a lake; green hills; a house in the background. The top left-hand corner shows an elderly black man, the top right-hand corner an elderly white man; they are set apart by the flag of South Africa that extends from the top centre to the film title in the very centre of the poster. Text is inscribed on the flag, providing further information about the two male characters the poster features.

SIMILARITIES	– Striking bisection of the upper parts of the posters – Thus establishment of a certain contrast (black v. white) – Title = eye-catcher – Landscape depicted (yet to a different degree)
DIFFERENCES	– Colouring (greyish-brownish v. very colourful; but cf. publication dates here) – Left: landscape/weather rather threatening (heavy wind, gathering storm clouds, fire) v. right: idyllic & peaceful (light, green, tree, lake) – Left: contrast between groups of people (of different skin colour) v. right: contrast between two men (of different skin colour) – Hint at a crime committed in the left poster – Inclusion of the South African flag in the right poster (only adopted in 1994, cf. release of the film in 1995)

6. **Keeping in mind the text excerpts, write an interview with one of the directors in which you ask about and assess the design of the poster.**

Individual answer; results from task 5 should be taken into consideration. An assessment of which one is more appropriate against the background of the given excerpts should become obvious in the interviewer's questions and the interviewee's answers.

7. **Refresh what you have learned about izibongo poetry in the first chapter. Then split into two groups and turn M 1a and M 1b into pieces of izibongo poetry. Give a performance in class!** SB p. 24

Individual answer; the religious-like character of the text excerpts should become apparent and an abundance of imagery should be used (cf. info box, SB p. 16). It would make sense to tell the poem from today's point of view in order to "conserve" the coming into being of the shantytowns, since izibongo is also a form of oral history.

8. Do further research on Khayelitsha, one of the largest townships in South Africa, located near Cape Town. Prepare a presentation on Khayelitsha, focusing on living conditions, problems, and attempts to alleviate the poor people's situation.

@ SNG-40657-007

Khayelitsha ist die zweitgrößte Township in Südafrika (nach Soweto, vgl. M 9) und befindet sich circa 25 km süd-östlich von Kapstadt. Der Name entstammt der Xhosa-Sprache und bedeutet ursprünglich „Neue Heimat". Verschiedene Seiten mit Informationen sind im Webcode zusammengefasst.

An dieser Stelle könnte sich (in Vorbereitung auf M 9, Aufg. 6) die Frage anschließen, ob vor dem Hintergrund der Verhältnisse in Khayelitsha der Erwerb von Eigentum dort lohnenswert und zukunftsträchtig erscheint. Im Internet finden sich zahlreiche Seiten, die Häuser in Khayelitsha feilbieten, zum Teil zu (für den ärmeren Teil der südafrikanischen Bevölkerung) nicht unerheblichen Preisen, siehe das Beispiel im Webcode.

M 2 Freedom from Oppression: 50 Years since the Group Areas Act

SAHA (South African History Archive)

SB p. 24

1. Describe the photograph provided here and state what the man in the picture is protesting against.
The photograph features a black man sitting in its centre foreground, wearing a light-coloured sweatshirt and a wide-brimmed hat. He has a sign attached to his back via his belt which says "It's my country. I will live where I choose to!!" In the background, one can see a crowd of people who are either also sitting or standing.
The man seems to be protesting against a forced relocation/resettlement since he demands freedom of residence in his own country.

2. Make an educated guess as to what the Group Areas Act said, based on your results from task 1.
Individual answer; students should mention that the man's slogan on the poster hints at a forced relocation of the black South Africans/a resettlement policy. Also, the name "Group Areas Act" suggests that this policy is not about individuals, but that it affects certain parts/groups of the population (so probably black South Africans).

SB p. 25

3. Write an entry for an encyclopaedia in which you describe the Group Areas Act of 1950, according to the text. Include a definition, its function for the white minority and the impact still felt today.
The Group Areas Act of 1950 divided the South African population into different racial groups and determined where people were allowed to live. Serving the purpose to consolidate apartheid, this meant that the lion's share of the land was given to the white population even though they were in the majority. Like this, the black population was not only excluded politically, but also economically, whereas the white minority retained and extended their privileges.
Even though the Group Areas Act was repealed in 1991, there are long-term impacts still felt today, since the homelands have become established as a means of ethnic

separation and still lag behind in terms of economic and social equality, which makes it harder to overcome apartheid for good.

4. **Against the backdrop of your encyclopaedia entry, present the Group Areas Act, its function and impact today to a German-speaking audience.**
Individual answer; the most important information (cf. task 3) should be included, but by no means merely "translated" one to one. Instead, the gist should be mediated.

5. **Write further protest slogans for the man shown in the photograph, based on the text. The man could, for example, decry the white minority's intentions, or he could also predict future consequences.**
Individual answers.

6. **Do further research on measures introduced by the apartheid governments intended to entrench "separate development", for example the Bantu Education Act No. 47 from 1953. Prepare short presentations and give them in class. Afterwards, make a timeline of apartheid measures and assess their impact on today's South Africa.**

Eine sehr detaillierte Auflistung und Klassifizierung findet sich im Webcode. Die Schüler können auch auf die Zeitleiste auf der Auftaktdoppelseite hingewiesen werden, die einige der wichtigsten Apartheid-Gesetze auflistet (u.a. den Bantu Education Act des Jahres 1953). Es bietet sich an, zu den wichtigsten Apartheid-„Stationen" zum Beispiel in Gruppen eine Wandzeitung anfertigen zu lassen, die während der Behandlung des Themas „Südafrika" im Klassenraum aufgehängt und auf die an mehreren Stellen verwiesen werden kann (vgl. z. B. M 3, Aufg. 5; M 4, Aufg. 4; M 12, Aufg. 2). Außerdem wäre nach der Besprechung ein Rückbezug auf Kapitel 1, M 1 sinnvoll, sodass die Schüler reflektieren, inwiefern das Apartheid-Regime als „Erblast" der Kolonisierung Südafrikas gesehen werden könnte.

SNG-40657-008 @

M3 Resolution 1761

The United Nations

1. **First, do some research on the organization of the UN and means the UN could and can make use of to work against threats to international peace and security.**

SB p. 26

Organization of the UN:
A chart can be found on the UN website, see Webcode.

SNG-40657-009 @

Means = Functions and Powers (of the Security Council):
Under the United Nations Charter, the functions and powers of the Security Council are:

- to maintain international peace and security in accordance with the principles and purposes of the United Nations;
- to investigate any dispute or situation which might lead to international friction;
- to recommend methods of adjusting such disputes or the terms of settlement;
- to formulate plans for the establishment of a system to regulate armaments;
- to determine the existence of a threat to the peace or act of aggression and to recommend what action should be taken;
- to call on Members to apply economic sanctions and other measures not involving the use of force to prevent or stop aggression;
- to take military action against an aggressor;
- to recommend the admission of new Members;
- to exercise the trusteeship functions of the United Nations in "strategic areas";

- to recommend to the General Assembly the appointment of the Secretary-General and, together with the Assembly, to elect the Judges of the International Court of Justice.

UN (ed.), Functions and Powers, www.un.org [15.01.2015]

2. In the following resolution, there is a strong focus on verbs that introduce ideas. Before reading, have a look at the verbs taken from the text and anticipate how the sentences are continued. Refer to what you have already learned about apartheid and about the UN.

Individual answer; all in all, the verbs hint at a rather reserved approach (cf. e. g. "to request") relying on member states' cooperation in the continued effort to implement sanctions (cf. e. g. "to recall", "to reaffirm"). However, it seems that the sanction has yet to be pronounced by the Security Council. Since one of the four declared main objectives of the UN was and is "[t]o help nations work together to improve the lives of poor people, to conquer hunger, disease and illiteracy, and to encourage respect for each other's rights and freedoms" [www.un.org/en/aboutun/index.shtml; 15.01.2015], apartheid would be something that must be tackled and overcome.

3. Scan the text to complete the sentence beginnings provided in task 1. Afterwards, give a summary of Resolution 1761.

Summary:

In the first part of the Resolution, previous resolutions are remembered that have called on the South African government to abandon its apartheid policy on the grounds that it endangers peace, and the behaviour of some UN member states is deplored that have given support to South Africa despite her policies.

In the second part of the Resolution, the continuing violations of the South African government are complained about, a government that has failed to comply with its obligations so far and thus works towards endangering peace, says the text.

Then, member states are called on to take measures against South Africa so that the system of apartheid and racial discrimination are overcome. These measures should, for example, comprise abandoning trade with South Africa by sea, land or air, and refraining from buying from or selling to South Africa. Furthermore, a Special Committee is to be established whose tasks are to keep South African policies under observation and to report to the Security Council.

Finally, the Security Council is called to action to implement measures, such as sanctions, against South Africa.

4. Explain why the General Assembly can only "request", but not "command" its member states and the Security Council to do something.

The General Assembly is the main representative body of the UN in which all member states are represented. It is the body that deliberates and negotiates UN policies, and it makes recommendations. However, it is the Security Council that decides if it calls on member states to impose economic sanctions, for example, or that can opt for military action (cf. task 1).

5. Discuss the effectiveness of the requested measures against South Africa's apartheid regime. Feel free to add further measures you can think of. You could also check out further measures introduced in order to give a more balanced assessment, cf. the webcode.

Individual answer; taking into consideration that the given Resolution was passed in 1962, and that apartheid was to last for another 22 years, it becomes quite obvious that the measures were not as successful as wished for. However, this is also due to the fact that in the time to come, member states would veto sanctions planned against South Africa, or would even support South Africa economically and militarily (cf. **Worksheet 4**, task 2, p. 61).

M 4 Appeal for Action against Apartheid

Chief Albert Luthuli & Reverend Dr Martin Luther King Jr.

1. **What could the two different solutions (cf. introduction) possibly consist of? Make an educated guess and, against the backdrop of Luthuli's and Martin Luther King Jr's short biographies, anticipate which solution the two of them might favour, and why.**

SB p. 29

Individual answer; basically, one can either use violence as a means to trigger change, or one could rely on peaceful means. The biographies of Luthuli and King indicate that the two of them would very likely favour a peaceful solution.

2. **State the first solution.**

The first solution would consist of a racial war against the race which persecuted all other races. Even though this might prove successful in the long run, it would severely limit the chances for an eventual unity among the races in South Africa.

3. **Turn the second solution into a speech to be given before the United Nations (cf. M 3) and present it.**

Content-wise, the speech should include:
- The call to "disciplined resistance"
- The demand to put pressure on the South African government from inside and outside the country to force them into complying with the demands of the non-white population and to overcome apartheid, namely:
  - to show action on Human Rights Day (10th December)
  - to ask governments abroad to agree to economic sanctions against South Africa and to enforce South Africa's isolation economically (for example by refraining from purchasing South African products)

Language-wise, the speech should:
- Create a connection to the audience by appealing to logos (their logical thinking/reason), pathos (the emotions of the audience) and ethos (i.e. the credibility and reliability of the speaker(s))
- Contain rhetorical devices aimed at stressing the message the speakers want to get across (e.g. rhetorical questions, anaphora, alliteration, antithesis, direct address, first person plural pronouns "we/our", etc.)

Nach der inhaltlichen Auseinandersetzung mit M 4 bietet es sich an, den möglichen Effekt der von Luthuli und King geforderten Maßnahmen kritisch zu beleuchten. Hier könnte ein Rückbezug zur Auftaktdoppelseite stattfinden, und zwar zu dem französischen Anti-Apartheid-Poster, das zu einem Boykott der Marke Outspan und ihrer sogenannten „Blutorangen" aufruft. Das französische Poster beruht auf der holländischen BOA, der Boycott Outspan Action der Jahre 1972/73, die in einem ersten Schritt über die Arbeitsbedingungen der südafrikanischen Arbeiter informierte und anschließend zu einem Boykott aufrief, der einer der erfolgreichsten seiner Art war.
Detaillierte Informationen über Ziele, Vorgehensweise und Erfolge der BOA finden sich im nebenstehenden Webcode.

SNG-40657-010 @

4. **Do further research on the Universal Declaration of Human Rights, adopted and proclaimed by the United Nations on 10 December 1948. Explain which articles were violated by apartheid.**

SB p. 30

The Universal Declaration of Human Rights was passed after the experiences of atrocities committed by Nazi Germany and the other fascist regimes, after the Second World War (1948). It was deemed necessary to prescribe once and for all what actually comprises the idea of inviolable human rights, which is why the Declaration is quite detailed, especially in comparison to former declarations of rights (cf. e.g. the American Declaration of Independence of 1776, or the French Declaration of the

Rights of Man and of the Citizen of 1789). The Declaration consists of a preamble and 30 Articles. Students will realize that apartheid basically violated all of the 30 Articles and could be asked to pick, for example, three Articles and give examples of how apartheid violated the respective Articles.
Example:

ARTICLE	VIOLATED BY APARTHEID B/C:
Article 1: All human beings are born free and equal in dignity and rights. They are endowed with reason and conscience and should act towards one another in a spirit of brotherhood.	– Apartheid entrenched "separate development", e. g. inferior education for black South Africans was established – The non-white majority was considered inferior by the white ruling class
Article 9: No one shall be subjected to arbitrary arrest, detention or exile.	– Detention was common practice (cf. M 10, M 11)
Article 13: (1) Everyone has the right to freedom of movement and residence within the borders of each state. (2) Everyone has the right to leave any country, including his own, and to return to his country.	– Anti-apartheid activists were put on trial, were banned or exiled (cf. e. g. Luthuli (p. 28), Biko (p. 42))

M 5 I Am Prepared to Die

Nelson Rolihlahla Mandela

SB p. 31

1. **[...] Taking into account what you know about the situation in South Africa from its colonisation up to the time the speech was delivered, come up with ideas on the ideal Mandela would die for.**
Individual answer; students could have a look at the timeline provided on the introductory pages for ideas and might refer to the ideal of racial and legal equality in South Africa/the abolishment of the apartheid policies/possibly also a take-over of power of the black majority/the fall of the white minority from power/their expulsion (cf. Mandela's political stance at the time of his trial as opposed to his later policy of reconciliation, SB p. 30).

2. **Describe the situation of the Africans and the reasons advanced by Mandela, and present his demands.**
Situation of the Africans:
Mandela describes South Africa as a country of contrasts between white and black South Africans. Whereas white South Africans are privileged and well-off, many black South Africans are restricted to regions of land that cannot be cultivated and are overcrowded. Also, many work on the land of and for the whites, and of those who have managed to live in the cities, there are still many who are subject to poverty.
Still the blacks rather complain about their legal situation which, says Mandela, is intended to keep the established privileges for the whites by denying the black South Africans the only solutions, which are education and gaining greater professional skills.

Mandela claims that the whites consider the blacks as inferior and even as a different and unhuman breed, denying them the same desires and emotions as they have. As one example of different and inhumane treatment Mandela refers to the Pass Laws.

Demands:

Basically, everything has to change in South Africa to eventually establish equality, for example as far as the payment of wages and the freedom to choose one's profession are concerned. Mandela lists several rights that are considered human rights, such as the freedom to choose one's residence, the possibility to live together with one's family, the freedom of movement and, all in all, a fair share of the country in all respects.

To Mandela, the most important demand is political equality even though the white minority might be afraid of this, since it is the only way to overcome the division of the country.

3. **Examine how Mandela tries to get his message across to his accusers. Focus on line of argument and rhetorical devices.**

Line of argument:

- ll. 1–11: introduction – outline/description of the situation the population of South Africa find themselves in
- ll. 12–17: remedies to solve the situation that is intended to be preserved by the whites
- ll. 18–35: establishing the contrast between white attitudes and black wants
- ll. 36–49: specification of the black population's demands and desires as the only remedy to the current grievances
- ll. 50–61: political equality as the cornerstone of change, even though feared by the white minority
- ll. 62–66: personal conclusion – ideals described before are worth living and dying for

Rhetorical devices, e.g.:

T(hesis)/Device	E(xample)	E(xplanation)
antitheses/ contrasts	e.g.: – "But it is a land of extremes ..." (l. 3) – "Yet most Africans ..." (l. 10) – "poor" v. "rich" (l. 12) – "White supremacy implies black inferiority." (l. 19) – cf. ll. 39 ff. etc.	– To stress the division of the country (white v. black, rich v. poor) – To illustrate the current situation of the blacks and the wished-for future
repetitions	e.g.: – "richest country/ies" (l. 1) – "white supremacy" (ll. 19, 20) – "the white man" (ll. 21, 52) [which is simultaneously a generalization, assuming all white Africans aim at subjugating the black in order to entrench the status quo)	– To draw attention to key ideas in the speech – To underline the importance of the whites' privileges in a country that is basically rich, but in which the riches are divided unfairly
enumeration	e.g.: – "labourers, labour tenants, and squatters" (l. 7)	– To stress to the menial labour that is the only option for the blacks because of white predominance

T(hesis)/Device	E(xample)	E(xplanation)
rhetorical questions	e. g.: – cf. l. 28	– To show the impossibility of climbing the social ladder for black South Africans – To make the audience linger and think about the issue in question to which no answer is necessary
parallelism & anaphora	e. g.: – cf. ll. 25 ff. – cf. ll. 39 ff. – cf. ll. 62 ff.	– To make the audience aware that black people are exactly as white people, driven by the same fears and hopes – To add urgency to black demands – To underscore his personal motivation and struggle in the fight for his ideal South African society, based on equality
first-person plural pronouns	e. g.: – cf. ll. 25 ff., 39 ff.	– To stress the demands of the group of the black population – To show that he does not speak up for himself only, but for the majority of South Africans
first-person personal/singular pronoun "I"	e. g.: – cf. l. 1, l. 31, ll. 62 ff.	– To show that he is personally affected by what he is talking about (not only because he is accused of a crime, but because he is talking about his personal ideal) – To convince his audience by ensuring them of his personal sacrifice for the ideals he has been talking about
?	?	?

4. **Explain in how far Mandela's last statement is a logical conclusion derived from his argumentation.**

On the one hand, his speech is structured in a clear and logical way (cf. analysis of the line of argument). On the other hand, Mandela creates a "frame" around his speech, since he begins by acknowledging to be "the First Accused" (l. 1), thus using the personal pronoun "I", which he again uses at the end of the speech when he declares that his lifetime struggle for equality is "an ideal for which [he is] prepared to die." (l. 66)

Thus the main part of his speech is dedicated to characterizing and decrying the state of affairs in South Africa and to outlining his vision of a future South Africa, guaranteeing racial unity and equality, so the ideal which he has been fighting for all his life and which seems worth dying for, too.

5. **Do further research on what Mandela was accused of and what he was eventually sentenced with. Then scan the speech one more time for possible reasons that would explain the harshness of the verdict.**

SB p. 32

Accusations/charges & background:

- Sabotage & conspiracy
- In June 1960, the ANC had decided against Mandela's proposal to use arms against the South African apartheid regimes, but eventually the military organ "Spear of the Nation " (Umkhonto we Sizwe) was established nevertheless
- In June 1961, Mandela sent a warning to South African newspapers, warning of a new campaign in case there was no national constitutional convention held; he retreated into the Rivonia hideout (that's why the trial is dubbed the 'Rivonia Trial') from where he and his supporters began to plan a sabotage campaign; these acts of sabotage followed in the next 18 months to come (e. g. lighting explosives, burning crops)
- After military training in Ethiopia in 1962, Mandela was arrested shortly after his return to South Africa

Sentence:

- Guilty on all charges
- Life imprisonment (however, the death sentence would also have been possible, which led Mandela to show a "thumbs-up" upon hearing the sentence; before, Alan Paton (cf. M 1) had spoken for the accused, which might have influenced the sentence)

Possible reasons:

Individual answer; students could point to the fact that Mandela was a well-known, respected and popular personality, that he was made out as the leading figure of the "Spear of the Nation", but also that his visions for a future South Africa would very likely be hitting the nail on the head as far as the fears of the white minority are concerned, who were afraid of a revolution and of being overpowered by the black majority in case they granted them equality on all levels (cf. ll. 50 ff.).

M 6 A Ripple of Hope

Robert Kennedy

1. **Have a look at the photograph, showing Senator Kennedy with African students. Collect suitable adjectives to describe the atmosphere captured in the picture. Relate your ideas to the title of the speech, "A Ripple of Hope".**

SB p. 33

Suitable adjectives, e. g.: positive, optimistic, joyful/joyous, excited, expectant, hopeful, etc. (so the atmosphere as captured in the photograph seems to correspond with the gist of the speech which has come to be known as the "ripple of hope" speech).

2. **[...] Revise what you know/remember about the American Civil Rights Movement, which was in full swing at the time the speech was given and which Kennedy supported. Which parallels to South Africa would you think possible?**

Individual answer; students should mention that in both cases, "separate development" was fostered and entrenched, but under a different label; also, in both cases black people were classified as "inferior" and excluded from participating in (white) public life (e. g. racial segregation in schools, public transportation, etc. → the so-called "Jim Crow Laws" – "separate but equal"). In the case of South Africa, it is striking that the black South Africans clearly outnumbered the ruling white class. Still, apartheid was in full swing by the time of the given speech, whereas the black Americans had already scored some important successes in their struggle for equality, such as Brown vs. Board of Education (1954), declaring segregated public schools illegal, or the Montgomery Bus Boycott of 1955 which eventually led to the Supreme Court ruling segregated public transportation unconstitutional. The March on Washington of 1963, led by Martin Luther King Jr., would eventually lead to the Civil Rights Act of 1964, outlawing discrimination and segregation based on race, nationality or gender. These achievements should also be taken into account when discussing task 5.

3. Summarise Kennedy's speech.

Kennedy starts off by describing the historic origins and current state of a country which he eventually concedes is the United States of America.

He then proceeds with elaborating on the issues already hinted at in the first part of his speech, stating that even though the USA has already worked on overcoming the inequality between classes and races, there still is left a lot to be improved. Kennedy says that millions of black Americans are not yet qualified for higher-skilled jobs even though there are some examples that can serve as beacons of hope, such as Martin Luther King, but these cannot make up for centuries of injustice that have left their mark.

In the following, Kennedy lists what the USA must do and why, namely establish equality in all respects simply because it is the right path to choose. Yet he also concedes that there are difficulties to be overcome, and that these problems do not exist in the USA alone, but that the USA's chosen way is to respect minority rights despite possible fears that minorities might be subjugated, especially in case their race differs from the one of the majority.

Kennedy concludes by acknowledging that the USA's chosen way will and cannot be imposed on other nations since the development of nations differs, but that in a quickly progressing world, freedom and justice for everyone must be benchmarks in order to cope with change efficiently.

4. Analyse the persuasive techniques Kennedy applies in order to win his audience over. In this context, also explain the function of the beginning of the speech (cf. ll. 1–7).

Function of the beginning:

- Making the audience believe he is talking about South Africa because of the obvious parallels to the history and current state of affairs in the USA/deliberately misleading the listeners ("I came here because of my deep interest and affection for a land ...", l. 1)
- Raising hopes among the (black) listeners who are aware of changes having taken place in the USA in the course of the American Civil Rights Movement (cf. task 2)
- Presenting himself as a reliable speaker/creating credibility since he knows what he is talking about ("ethos")
- Comic relief by revealing the described country to be the USA, also underlined by him saying "of course" (l. 7)

→ All in all, it is striking that Kennedy never addresses the situation in South Africa directly, but merely establishes parallels between the USA and South Africa (not only in the beginning of the speech). Thus the audience is constantly reminded that the USA – despite facing similar "challenges" to "white supremacy" – has already made concessions which, in consequence, would also be possible in South Africa without entailing the feared "revolution" the white minority was afraid of. Kennedy words his speech very carefully, trying to avoid clashes with South Africa's apartheid regime. One further example of this would be his concession that the path chosen by the USA might not work for other nations because of different developments (cf. ll. 40 ff.). However, before saying so, Kennedy more or less directly addresses the fear of South Africa's white minority of being subjugated by the black majority (cf. ll. 33 ff.), a fear which he exposes to be unsubstantiated in case nations work towards freedom and justice, which in his conclusion he considers indispensable in times of quick change and development (cf. ll. 42). Thus his conclusion can be considered a(n) (indirect) call to action to the South African government to introduce change as otherwise they will not be able to compete with other nations in the long run.

(Further) persuasive techniques:

- First-person singular pronouns "I"/"my" to show his interest and involvement (cf. e.g. ll. 1, 7, 8, etc.)
- First-person plural pronouns "we"/"our" to exemplify what his country has already done and will do in the future (and could thus serve as an example) (cf. e.g. ll. 11, 21, etc.)
- Frequent use of enumerations to show the contrast between what has already been done and what still needs to be done (cf. ll. 21–23), also underlined by antitheses/contrasts (cf. ll. 25 ff., 34 ff.)
- Giving specific and well-known examples of "success stories" to show that everything is possible (the American Dream) (cf. ll. 17 ff.)
- Use of parallelism/anaphora to underscore what needs to be done, and for which reasons the USA believes so (cf. ll. 24 ff., 35 ff.)
- Imagery of nations "march[ing] to the beat of different drummers" (l. 41) to illustrate his thesis that nations develop at a different pace on the one hand, and to visualize that there is an external force that drives everyone on the other hand

5. **Also referring to the given photograph, discuss why this speech raised hopes among the black South Africans.**

Individual answers; analysis results (especially the parallels drawn between South Africa and the USA, cf. task 4) should be taken into consideration, as well as the fact that Kennedy also visited homelands such as Soweto.

6. **[...] Watch the trailer online and compare the atmosphere created with the one in the photograph and in the speech itself.** SB p. 34

Photograph & Speech	Trailer
– photograph: crowd of people cheering for Kennedy; smiling faces; extending their arms to touch him/shake hands with him; overwhelmingly positive/optimistic/expectant & joyful – speech: positive but more wary; careful/indirect way of addressing change in SA, but ends on a positive/optimistic note	– trailer: positive in general but also melancholic and sentimental (e.g. the people shown named after him, piano music playing, African singing); qualifying remarks about his visit in Soweto elevate his position (also cf. comments, "first time somebody told them they were a human being"; "wanted me to live like a king" or the comments by Kennedy's brother); specific quotations from speeches underlined by fade-in text ("words that mattered then and now") also serve to single Kennedy out as one of the great political leaders of his time
→ All in all, the atmosphere in the trailer is a more dramatic and sentimental one, lacking the blissful and positive one conveyed especially in the photograph and, with restrictions mentioned above, in the speech itself. The film trailer of course intends to attract the potential viewers to watch the whole documentary and thus attempts to underline the singularity of Kennedy's visit (especially to Soweto) and his speeches as a contribution to the fight against apartheid (also cf. the title of the documentary as such) and as part of the legacy of the Kennedy family in general. The sentimentality of the atmosphere can also be explained when taking into consideration that the makers of the documentary were well aware of the fact that Kennedy was to be assassinated only two years after his visit to South Africa.	

M7 My Beautiful Land

Antjie Krog

SB p. 35

1. […] If you could build yourself the land of your dreams, what would it look and be like? […] What would/do you cherish about a land?
Individual answer; starting out from their personal lives, students would probably mention personal freedoms (e.g. of opinion, movement, religions, etc.) as well as human and civil rights in general which they are endowed with (and which could not be taken for granted in apartheid South Africa).

2. Describe the speaker's "beautiful land" and point out the message of the poem.
The speaker's "beautiful land" is a land without apartheid, a land in which white and black people can live peacefully together, love each other and start a family without being threatened or persecuted.
The message of the poem is that, through mutual understanding, trust and respect, the young South Africans shall "bring peace and love" to their country, contrary to what the old hardliners in parliament ("verkramp … goat face[s]") are holding fast to.

3. Examine the structure the poet makes use of to illustrate the gap between the present and the envisaged future.
The poem is worded in a seemingly very simple but also effective way. The very first stanza introduces the idea that the country the speaker dreams of is merely a wish and in the future, since the speaker has to "build" the land, implying that it does not yet exist. The features of this land of the speaker's dreams are introduced by a recurrent "where" (cf. ll. 2, 4, 6, 9, etc.). Since these features seem to be in the future, they allow conclusions about the present state: skin colour does count (cf. l. 2), the government issues restrictions (cf. ll. 4f.), marriage is a necessary prerequisite for love (cf. l. 8), and in general, interracial love is a legal and/or societal problem.

4. The poem was originally written in Afrikaans, and not until the year 2000 did Krog publish the English translation. Discuss in how far this possibly changes the way in which the poem was received at the time of its publication, and why.
Individual answers.

5. The German Board of Education is planning a special anthology dealing with poetry published during apartheid in South Africa. Write a letter to the person in charge in which you recommend "My Beautiful Land" as an excellent contribution to the anthology.
Individual answer; students might want to refer to the poet's origins, the message of the poem, the language it was originally published in, the time of publication, addressees, issues addressed, etc.

M8 The Smell of Apples

Mark Behr

SB p. 36

1. Marnus's father claims that "all the best blacks were taken away by the slave merchants." (ll. 7/8). […] With the help of the map provided, explain how the system of Triangular Trade worked. Then make an educated guess as to why the character makes reference to earlier forms of trade.
Triangular Trade (*Dreieckshandel*):
The system of the Triangular Trade was introduced by Britain for the benefit of the American colonies (before their 1776 independence from Britain, of course) and Brit-

ain as the mother country. Simply speaking, this system provided the American colonies with slaves from Africa to work the plantations, the raw materials (such as tobacco, sugar) from the plantations were then shipped to Britain, where the materials were manufactured into goods and in turn traded in for slaves from Africa, or shipped back to the American colonies. Thus there was a constant influx of slaves that were brought from Africa to the North American continent.
Educated guess:
Individual answer; students could assume that Marnus's father might complain about the "drain" of people capable of performing hard physical work inflicted on Africa during the time of the Triangular Trade, for example.

2. Outline the father's argumentation. Relate your results to task 1.
First, the father presumes the world to be South Africa's enemy because of the country's riches and its strategically important geographical position. Next, he accuses other countries of taking South Africa's treatment of the blacks as a pretext to make them pariahs whereas others have done worse but just veil it, in contrast to South Africa.
Marnus's father then claims the intelligent blacks have been taken away from Africa to America and turned into slaves which, says he, has left only unintelligent ones behind. That is why the USA thinks they are superior and entitled to tell South Africa what to do, like the rest of the world that incites the black South Africans.
The father closes his argumentation by stating that South Africa's army stands strong and that support by Portuguese colonies around Africa is available.

3. Analyse the way Mark Behr presents the characters to the reader. Focus on narrative perspective.
As provided in the introduction to the text, the excerpt (and the whole novel as such) is narrated by eleven-year-old Marnus Erasmus, a white Afrikaner, who is eavesdropping while his father, a high-ranking army general, is having a conversation with another general. In the given excerpt, it does not become clear though that the story is narrated in the first person.
Thus the first-person narrator, Marnus's point of view, is limited to this character's thoughts, feelings and observations, which is why the reader merely learns about the father as he is seen and observed through Marnus's eyes. The given narrative perspective is thus highly subjective and the reader tends to identify and sympathize with the character, since he/she (the reader) lacks access to the thoughts, feelings and observations of other characters who might put the first-person narrator's remarks into perspective.
The narrative perspective thus only tells us about the father's highly controversial and racist remarks from the perspective of a child who is not yet able to evaluate this difficult topic and who is easily influenced, especially since the father is a person that is most likely admired by the child. Also, the introduction to the text provides the information that the child is indeed indoctrinated by his father. That means that the judgement and putting into perspective of the father's statements is left to the reader alone since the son is unqualified to do so, which is further underlined by the fact that the father's conversational partner does not make any contributions to the talk.

4. Put yourself into the shoes of the General listening to the father's remarks. Write his reply in which you counter his arguments. Make ample use of your knowledge gained about South Africa so far.
Individual answer; since students are asked to "counter" the father's racist remarks, the general should argue from a humanist perspective, e. g. reminding the father of the UN Declaration of Human Rights of 1948 (cf. M 4, task 4), by stressing the invio-

lability and inalienability of human rights, by exposing the ridiculousness of the father's argumentation (cf. e. g. the Triangular Trade argument), etc.

Hier sei angemerkt, dass es sich bei dem „General" im Roman tatsächlich um einen chilenischen General handelt, den Marnus „Mr. Smith" nennen soll und über dessen Besuche er von seinem Vater zu Verschwiegenheit verpflichtet wird. Da dieser General im vorliegenden Textauszug nicht zu Wort kommt, könnten ihm die Schüler durchaus die humanistische Perspektive in den Mund legen, sollten aber darauf hingewiesen werden, dass dies im Gesamtkontext des Romans betrachtet nicht als wahrscheinlich gelten kann.
Die Schüler könnten weiterführend den Putsch in Chile im Jahre 1973 recherchieren, der Allende stürzte und Pinochet an die Macht brachte – was der chilenische General in einem positiven Licht sieht. Daran könnte sich vor dem Hintergrund des vorliegenden Textauszugs die Frage anschließen, was Marnus' Vater, der ebenfalls ein General ist, und sein Besucher wohl zu besprechen haben könnten.

M 9 Soweto

M 9a Die Analphabetin, die rechnen konnte

Jonas Jonasson

SB p. 37

1. [...] With a partner, talk about the pictures. How do they make you feel?
Individual answers.

SB p. 38

2. [...] How could it be possible to use irony/sarcasm when speaking about 16 June? Whose side would probably be ridiculed?
From today's perspective, the only side whose behaviour might be ridiculed can be the side of the apartheid regime that used violent means to put down the uprising. Sarcasm implies saying the opposite of what you really mean in order to utter harsh criticism. That is why using sarcasm when speaking about 16 June can indeed be considered appropriate since this rhetorical device exposes the ridiculousness of the regime's proceedings while simultaneously expressing sympathy for the more than reasonable demands of the students.

3. Find and explain examples of irony/sarcasm in the excerpt.

He says:	He means:
– „[...] regte sich eine Menge Schüler über die neueste Idee der Regierung auf [...]." (ll. 1 f.)	– *sich aufregen* = understatement since the students went on the streets to protest; *neueste Idee* implying that also preceding "ideas" or measures were ridiculous; use of the word *Idee* makes the government's proceeding appear spontaneous/not well-planned
– „Sie fanden, dass es doch wesentlich leichter war, etwas zu lernen [...]." (ll. 4–6)	– Stating the obvious and thus showing the reasonable quality of the students' complaints
– „lauschte mit Interesse [...] typisch für die südafrikanische Ordnungsmacht [...] eröffnete das Feuer" (ll. 9–12)	– Saying the opposite of what is meant (*mit Interesse*) and adding a bitter tone when speaking about the reaction of the government and labelling it as "typical"

– „hob die Polizei den Austausch der Argumente auf ein ganz anderes Niveau“ (l. 15)	– Playing on the common assumption that “putting something on a different level” is rather connoted positively and deconstructing this notion by pointing at the intensified use of armaments against one’s own people
– „Das Schulamt [...] stark zurückgegangen waren.“ (ll. 17–19)	– Exposing the cunningness of the South African regime that can even make profit from killing its own people

4. Evaluate if it is appropriate to use sarcasm when speaking about 16 June. In your evaluation, also refer back to the pictures provided.
Individual answer.

An dieser Stelle könnte nochmals der Rückbezug zum ersten Kapitel stattfinden, und zwar zu Mark Twains Beschreibung der Rhodes’schen Methoden (M 3), da auch Twain sich durch einen sehr sarkastischen Schreibstil auszeichnet. Daher stellt sich auch hier die Frage nach der Angemessenheit des Gebrauchs von Ironie/Sarkasmus.

M 9b Im Ghetto von Soweto (Auntie’s House)

Joy Denalane

1. Have a look at the various stills from the music video of “Im Ghetto von Soweto”. What kind of song do you expect with regard to a) the lyrics and b) the mood expressed? Briefly talk to a partner. SB p. 39
Individual answers; students should point at the fact that the stills represent an ambiguous picture of Soweto: poverty/homelessness is contrasted with tradition/pride/family.

2. Describe the memories and experiences the speaker connects with Auntie Jane’s, Auntie Nancy’s and Auntie Eve’s houses in Soweto.

Auntie Jane:	the speaker recalls the police force shooting school children in 1976, one of these school children she calls by name (Pieterson)
Auntie Nancy:	this house evokes memories of the Pass Laws and of putting people in detention where they were tortured and from which some would not emerge anymore
Auntie Eve:	Eve’s house is connected with sickness and disease, formerly tuberculosis, now HIV and AIDS

Mit „’84 in Diepkloof“ bezieht sich Denalane auf die Inhaftierung der gesamten COSAS-Führung (Congress of South African Students) in Diepkloof, einer Township Johannesburgs.

3. Explain why this song can be categorized as a protest song. Refer to both the stills from the video and to the lyrics.
Definition:
“A protest song is a song which is associated with a movement for social change and hence part of the broader category of topical songs (or songs connected to current events). It may be folk, classical, or commercial in genre. Among social movements that have an associated body of songs are the abolition movement, women’s suffrage, the labor movement, civil rights, the anti-war movement, the feminist move-

ment, animal rights movement, vegetarianism and veganism, and environmentalism."

"Protest Song", http://en.wikipedia.org/wiki/Protest_song [23.01.2015]

Denalane's song can be categorized as a protest song because the lyrics deplore the current state of affairs in Soweto that is traced back to Soweto's history of violence (cf. 16 June, first stanza), suppression/unlawful treatment of the native people (cf. Pass Laws and detention, second stanza) and the impact disease and sickness had and have, especially on the poorer parts of the population living in Soweto (cf. tuberculosis and HIV/AIDS, third stanza). Thus today's conditions are presented as a legacy of the past, which simultaneously calls for social change.
However, the stills also show a positive side of Soweto even though they also represent the downside as captured in the lyrics (cf. homeless person in rubble and white person walking by). Despite the criticism uttered, Soweto is also characterized by tradition (cf. still featuring people in traditional costumes), family (cf. still on the bottom right) and pride (cf. giant "Soweto" letters people are gathered around).

CD 1

4. **Listen to the song and examine how the musical orchestration supports the message the artist wants to convey. Make use of the language support provided.**

MESSAGE	MUSICAL ORCHESTRATION, e.g.:
The people of Soweto stand together despite the burdens of the past and the present which they must endure.	The music is ... – rhythmic/powerful/energetic/... The music ... – creates a feeling of (both happiness and sadness established through the contrast between the rhythm that makes one clap along and the content) The song has ... – a catchy melody/rhythm. The mood is ... – moving/disturbing/... The singer's voice is ... – deep/soothing/...
→ The ambivalent message of the song is mirrored in the musical orchestration.	

Hier bietet es sich als Alternative zu einem reinen Hörauftrag auch an, diesen um das Musikvideo zu erweitern. Ein möglicher Hör-Seh-Auftrag wäre, die Schüler die Stills kontextualisieren und den Bezug zu den Lyrics herstellen zu lassen.

SB p. 40

5. **Turn the lyrics into a speech to be given before the South African Truth and Reconciliation Commission (cf. chapter 3). Think of at least three rhetorical devices you could use to make your speech convincing to your audience. Make notes only and rehearse your speech before giving it in class.**
Individual answer; results from task 2 should be taken into consideration (see comment on M 4, task 3 for language requirements)

SB p. 41

6. **Do further research on Soweto today. If you could make a visit to South Africa, would you go and visit Soweto? Give reasons for your choice.**
Individual answers.

Auch heute ist die Township Soweto (vgl. SB, S. 37) von Armut und Gewalt geprägt, zum Beispiel wurden erst im Januar 2015 mindestens 121 Menschen dort von der Polizei inhaftiert, nachdem es zu Angriffen gegen und Plünderungen von Geschäften und Häusern von Ausländern in Johannesburg gekommen war.
Dennoch gibt es die Möglichkeit, die südafrikanischen Townships, unter anderem Soweto, im Rahmen eines Tagesauflugs zu besichtigen. Den Schülern könnte bei der Bewertung

zum Beispiel der Gegensatz zwischen „Armentourismus" und „Unterstützungsmaßnahme" aufgezeigt werden, oder es könnte auch die Frage nach dem Voyeurismus ausländischer Touristen gestellt werden, die sich sozusagen als „Peeping Toms" die Lebensbedingungen in den Townships anschauen.
Touren buchen kann man z. B. auf dieser Website: www.soweto.co.za.

M 10 Cry Freedom

M 10a Biko – Cry Freedom

1. Outline the argumentation of the accusers and of the defence. SB p. 42

Accusers: by inviting the black community to think for themselves, the Black Consciousness Movement threatens to overthrow the South African government's monopoly on truth.
Defence: Blacks have long been fed up with being oppressed by the white apartheid regime, and it is time for them to call for freedom of thought and speech and gain more self-confidence within the political realities of the regime.

2. Explain how Woods exposes the accusations as ridiculous.

Woods explains the wording of the prosecution by using clarifying phrases like "That is to say" and "in a sense" to expose that the concept of freedom of thought is not granted those on trial. Freedom of thought, however, is the indispensable condition of nearly every other form of freedom, thus must not be interpreted as an act of "subversion". Subsequently, calling the Black Consciousness philosophy "a danger to public safety" and the cause of "racial confrontation" must be understood as irony. In reality, it is vice versa: it is the white apartheid regime's philosophy that fosters discrimination, political corruption and the percussions of violence. So the accusations are unmasked as ridiculous in that they are extremely silly, even absurd, i.e., preposterous to reason.

M 10b Cry Freedom: The Courtroom Scene

1. Copy the graphic visualisation provided here. Then sum up the gist of the debate between the prosecutor and Biko. SB p. 43

BIKO	**PROSECUTION**
Argument 1: In a plural society like South Africa all people shall live and prosper together.	
	Reaction: But how can they live together when, as you maintain, the white government exerts "naked terrorism"?

Reaction:
What I mean by "naked terrorism" is the direct and indirect violence non-white people are confronted with every day. This constitutes more terrorism than the words these men have been charged for.

Reaction:
But when you talk about your "true leaders", you refer to black men that have called for violence against the South African government.

Reaction:
What these men have in common is that they have stood up for the black community and infused them with pride in themselves.

Reaction:
So you answer to what you call "naked terrorism" by provoking violence in the black community?

Reaction:
No, our movement does not seek violence.

Reaction:
But you yourself have called for "direct confrontation".

Reaction:
Confrontation with opposing ideas can take place non-violently.

Reaction:
But your criticism of the white government will lead to violence as it will no doubt inflame racial hatred and anti-whiteism.

Reaction:
Blacks have long endured hardships. We want them to stop accepting them, to confront them. We encourage them to develop hope for themselves and the country. Black Consciousness centres around us alone, without consideration of Whites.

@ SNG-40657-011

In einem seltenen Interview, das Steve Biko kurz vor seiner Ermordung gab, spricht er ausführlich über die Black Consciousness Bewegung (s. Webcode).

2. **State the judge's contribution to the scene.**

The judge interrupts the debate between Biko and the prosecutor by stating that none of the documents he has at hand show anything positive said about the white government. His second contribution is a question he asks Biko, namely the question if Biko accusing the white government of doing only very little good adds to increasing anti-white sentiments and aggravating the hatred between the races.

3. **[...] Explain the role he plays here. Consider your results from task 2 in your explanation.**
In this scene, the judge is the interrogator. The basis of this interrogation is documents published by the Black Consciousness Movement, including Steve Biko. The judge frequently quotes from these documents, trying to clarify the authors' intentions. In his quest for certainty the judge makes further inquiries on how to understand the philosophy of the movement. After all, it is his duty to assure himself if the men have advocated violence and have thus committed a criminal offence or not. Throughout the interrogation the judge behaves with integrity and restraint.

4. **Examine how the following contrasts are emphasised in the given text: white v. black/ state v. the individual/(white) system v. (black) consciousness/prosecutor v. Biko.**
White v. black:
- Biko wants a South Africa where both white and black shall live together, but recognizes the necessary struggle of the blacks for survival in a time when the white government does nothing good
- The judge voices his concern that Biko's approach might increase anti-white sentiments among the blacks
- Joint efforts seem to be pointless

State v. the individual:
- People who speak up for the demands are violently beaten down by the policy representing the executive branch of government & state
- The government's treatment of the blacks (e. g. townships) resembles terrorism, says Biko, and the individual does not stand a chance because those who speak out are tried for it

(White) system v. (black) consciousness:
- The system endorses and entrenches "separate development" and denies blacks human rights as well as hopes
- Black consciousness creates awareness for the misdoings of the white system ("naked terrorism") and seeks to end it
- Black consciousness cherishes individuality and the plurality of society whereas the white system pursues a policy of "bringing into line" and keeping down the black population

Prosecutor v. Biko:
- The two opponents in this courtroom scene which simultaneously represent all the other contrasts examined above in person

5. **In the film, the director Richard Attenborough clearly encourages his viewers to side with Biko by means of cinematic devices, such as camera work. Write a storyboard for the person operating the camera. [...]**
Individual answer; analysis results should be taken into consideration, especially the established contrasts. In order to portray Biko in a favourable way, the students could have the person operating the camera use eye-level shots and close-ups, for example. The accusers could be shown from low angle to underline their alleged superiority.

6. **In groups of three, prepare a dramatic reading of the script. [...] Give a performance in class!** SB p. 44
Individual answer.

7. **The following film still shows Denzel Washington as Biko at the dock. Describe his facial expression and his body language in general.** SB p. 45
Washington alias Biko appears carefree and calm despite the stressful and threatening situation. Posture, smile and gesture reinforce this impression. Obviously, he feels confident and safe while eloquently advocating the Black Consciousness philosophy. That is why students should rather pick adjectives from the positive semantic field, such as "blithe" or "determined".

8. **Against the backdrop of the text, explain which line would fit best to the given still. Give reasons for your choice.**
Individual answer; the body language as captured in the given still as well as the facial expressions indicate that a decisive statement is being made, such as ensuring the jury that Black Consciousness does not want violence, or pointing at the hardships black South Africans have to endure in their own country.

M 10c Cry Freedom: The Ending

SB p. 46

1. **Revise what you said about the mood contained in *Nkosi sikelel' iAfrika*. Starting from there, what kind of ending do you expect for *Cry Freedom*, and why?**
Individual answer; the students are, however, expected to recur to the Christian aspect of love, forgiveness and hope.

2. **Check the short biographical account of Biko to find out about the way he found his untimely end. Relate your findings to task 1.**
The way Biko died (cf. comment on task 4) makes love, forgiveness and hope hard to realize.
However, although the major conflict between the black South African population and the ruling white South African government is not resolved as the list of prison deaths indicates all too painfully, the film ends on a positive note. This is due to *Nkosi sikelel' iAfrika*, which foreshadows the change of the political situation (with Nelson Mandela's release) and the subsequent dismantling of the system of apartheid.

3. **Taking turns with a partner or in a group, read out the official explanations for the deaths in detention. What is your impression of the official explanations? Was this impression reinforced by the reading-out-loud activity?**
Individual answer; The students will certainly feel that reading out loud will intensify the horror of all those covert assassinations, perpetrated under false pretences.

4. **Unmask the absurdity of these official explanations by comparing the way Biko died with what was officially said.**
Biko is said to have gone on a hunger strike that led to his death. In reality, however, he died from a severe brain haemorrhage after having been tortured in detention. The reason for his arrest and subsequent death was a relatively marginal one: he was unauthorized to enter a part of town prohibited for blacks but had ignored the prohibition.

M 11 In Detention

Christopher van Wyk

SB p. 47

1. **When people were put in detention, this basically meant imprisonment without trial. Look up a definition of *habeas corpus* and explain why the South African policies violated human and international rights with that.**
Definition:
The Latin *phrase habeas* corpus literally means "you shall have the body". In practice, it means that somebody who has been arrested and put in detention has the right to defend him-/herself in a court of law, so it is an instrument against arbitrary arrest and imprisonment.

South African policies:
Detention without trial was one of the most appalling of the South African apartheid regime's methods of social control. They violated human and international rights under the pretence of securing law and order, but in reality they just struggled to ensure white supremacy. They could do so in an unhampered way because Black Consciousness was not on the rise yet.

2. **Taking turns with a partner or in a group, read out the verses of the poem. What is your impression? Was this impression reinforced by the reading-out-loud activity? Compare your ideas with M 10c.**
Individual answer.

3. **As described in the introduction to the text, this poem indirectly comments on the number of deaths in detention. Make an educated guess as to why open criticism would have been a daring venture at the time the poem was published, also taking the author's background into consideration.**
Individual answer; the students are, however, expected to find out that van Wyk humorously plays with words. His is a non-threatening strategy though an effective one as laughter can make a difference, more than a tone of serious venom (also cf. M9a, sarcasm as a weapon). This was especially important when considering the author's background, being a black poet writing in a time when apartheid was in full swing and freedom of speech severely curtailed. Thus he veils his message in his indirect comments on deaths in detention – a threat he might also have been faced with.

4. **With reference to M 10c, illustrate why "In Detention" is an example of satire.**
The poet quotes a series of statements from the prison authorities announcing the deaths of black prisoners. "He fell from the ninth floor" (l. 6), for instance, is an absurd excuse because a handcuffed prisoner can hardly climb through barred prison windows. Equally absurd is "He slipped on a piece of soap" (l. 3) as a cause of death since a prisoner is very unlikely to fatally strike his head on a slippery floor. By presenting the authentic excuses and playing around with them, i. e. mixing each with the other, van Wyk reveals their stupidity and presumptuousness in a satirical way.

5. **Examine how the poet exposes the true nature of deaths in detention by creating a growing absurdity in content and grammar. Focus on semantic violations (cf. e.g. l. 13) and the arrangement of transitive and intransitive verbs (cf. box on p. 48).**
The poem starts with three of the most common official explanations for deaths in detention: (1) suicide by hanging oneself, (2) fatal accident by falling from a great height, and (3) fatal accident by slipping and striking one's head. These three explanations are repeated without any alterations, only the order of presentation changes (cf. ll. 4–6). In the following lines (cf. ll. 7–14), however, the poet starts mixing the elements of the first three sentences, a technique by which he gives the initial explanations new, partly funny (e.g. "He slipped on the ninth floor while washing", l. 10), and partly nonsensical (e.g. "He washed from the ninth floor while slipping", l. 13) meanings. Each of the 14 lines begins with "He", followed by a verb. Apart from one verb ("He hanged himself"), the verbs are intransitive ones, among them the strange formulation "He hung" (e.g. l. 9), which could indicate that the prisoner was hanged by an unknown agent. This is contrasted by "He hanged himself" (e.g. l. 2), "to hang oneself" being a transitive verb. Here the object "himself", a reflexive pronoun, is the same person as the subject, which implies that the agent ("He") is to hold the blame for the action "hanged". This contrast, as well as repetition ("hanged" and "hung" occur in six lines) combined with mixing, highlight the unsettling tone of the poem.

M 12 Apartheid and the People of South Africa

SB p. 48

1. Describe the main findings depicted in the figures.

The figures show the impact apartheid had on the white and black population of South Africa, differentiating between various areas of life.

Whereas blacks constitute 19 million and whites only 4.5 million of the population, only 13 percent of the land is allocated to blacks, but 87 percent to whites. Similarly, 75 percent of the whites share the nation's national income, but only a low percentage of blacks do. What is also striking is that only one out of 44,000 blacks is a doctor, whereas 1 out of only 400 whites has learned this profession. Not only is the infant mortality rate much higher among blacks, with differences between the urban and the rural population, but also the annual expenditure on education per white pupil exceeds that spent on a black pupil by roughly 650 rands, with one teacher taking care of 22 white pupils and one responsible for 60 black pupils in comparison.

2. Revise what you have learned about measures introduced by the apartheid regimes in South Africa that were intended to entrench apartheid. Against this backdrop, assess the efficiency of these measures, as seen in the figures.

Apartheid measures: cf. M 2, task 6 + timeline, introductory pages

Efficiency:

Since there is a stark contrast between blacks and whites in all areas of life covered by the figures, one must assume that the measures indeed were effective in entrenching "separate development". In this context, the sanctions imposed on South Africa must also be seen critically as far as their efficiency is concerned.

3. Seeing that the end of apartheid would become reality twelve years later, take your results from tasks 1 and 2 and your knowledge gained so far about South Africa into consideration to make predictions about problems to be faced in the aftermath of apartheid.

Individual answer; against the backdrop of M 12, students might name economic disparities such as income gaps, educational disparities, restitution claims (of land, cf. additional text, subchapter 1); further ideas might centre on cries for revenge/retaliation, expulsion of the white minority from the country/government, etc.

M 13 Nobel Prize Acceptance Speech

Desmond Tutu

CD 2

SB p. 49

1. Before listening: Desmond Tutu does not begin his speech immediately, but instead calls his relatives and colleagues on stage to perform a traditional African song. [...] Make an educated guess as to the function of this introduction and ending.

On the one hand, the singing provides a frame for the speech. On the other hand, it creates a solemn and celebratory atmosphere. This is because the anthem as such is one of forgiveness, asking for God's blessing for all (religious) parts of the African society (cf. M 1a, task 5). Also, in 1984 the song was considered the secret national anthem of South Africa, representing her native peoples. Thus one can assume that to Tutu, the time is ripe for justice and reconciliation of the South African nation.

The fact that Tutu's family and friends and colleagues sing the song on stage, and that he also sings along, contributes to the solemnity of the moment.

Listening: cf. **Worksheet 3a/b**.

2. **After having listened to the speech, put yourself into the shoes of a supporter of the British Anti-Apartheid Movement (cf. M 14). Give a speech in which you comment on the way Tutu sketches South Africa's future.**
Individual answer; the supporter of the British Anti-Apartheid Movement would certainly be in favour of Tutu believing in God's support of change in South Africa, and he/she would surely agree with the way the current state of affairs is described. However, he/she might find the speech too vague and would probably opt for more concrete ways for how change could be achieved.

In seiner Nobel Lecture am Folgetag (11. Dezember 1984) analysiert Tutu die Situation in Südafrika noch sehr viel detaillierter (s. Webcode). An dieser Stelle bietet sich auch der Einsatz des Spiegel-Interviews mit Tutu auf ***Worksheet 4*** *an, aus dem Tutus Zukunftsvorstellungen klar hervorgehen.*

SNG-40657-012 @

M 14 Nelson Mandela Tribute Concert

The British Anti-Apartheid Movement

1. **Revise what you have learned about international sanctions and other measures imposed against the South African apartheid regime. Against this backdrop and the pictures provided here, discuss how effective a tribute concert of that extent could possibly have been.**
Individual answer; seeing that the UN's resolutions and sanctions had obviously failed to bring South Africa to her knees and abolish apartheid, students might advance the argument that a concert of such extent would most certainly draw the world public's attention to the situation once more, and that it would reach people who, before, had not been politicized to an extent that they would actively try to bring about change. The pure length of the concert (11.5 hours), the spectrum of countries watching (67) and its 600 million viewers makes it seem almost impossible to ignore. So international pressure was put on South Africa to rethink releasing Nelson Mandela from prison.

SB p. 50

2. **Do further research on Nelson Mandela's way "from terrorist to icon". Design a timeline that contains your main findings. If possible, add pictures, too.**
Individual answers.

Die Zeitleiste könnte z. B. unter der Wandzeitung (vgl. Kommentar zu M 2, Aufg. 6) aufgehängt werden. So werden die Bezüge zwischen Mandelas Biografie und den Maßnahmen der Apartheid-Regimes noch deutlicher.

M 15 Long Walk to Freedom

Nelson Mandela

1. **Watch the original footage, showing Mandela – accompanied by then-wife Winnie Mandela – walking through cheering ANC members. Make a list of suitable adjectives to describe the atmosphere in the streets and – based on your results – assess the importance of this moment (not only) for black South Africans. What would they probably expect from Mandela: Retribution or reconciliation?**
Suitable adjectives, e.g.:

- joyous, exhilarating, apprehensive (cf. introduction to video footage)
- excited, expectant, optimistic, exuberant
- tense

SB p. 51

Assessment of the importance of the moment:
The atmosphere clearly suggests that something grand is about to happen, that the tide has turned. The gathered crowds seem to be aware of that, too, trying to touch Mandela and hanging on his lips when he is speaking. There are both black and white people cheering him on, which also hints at a change in direction.
Retribution or reconciliation:
Individual answer; however, since Mandela says "I greet you all in the name of peace, democracy and freedom for all", it is more likely that he will pursue a policy of reconciliation rather than retribution.

2. **[...] Make an educated guess as to what to expect from Mandela's future policies: Retribution or reconciliation?**
Individual answer; students might hypothesize that Mandela harboured bitterness against the South African authorities because of his long imprisonment and because of the policies of apartheid (but students should also be asked what would speak for him believing in "reconciliation", too).

3. **Have a look at M 12, task 3 again. Against this backdrop, anticipate which problems Nelson Mandela was facing when taking over the South African presidency in 1994, and how he would intend to solve these.**
Cf. M 12, comment on tasks 1–3; ideas from tasks 1 and 2 should be taken into consideration.

4. **Outline Mandela's plan for a future South Africa and point out the reasons he gives for his attitude towards white South Africans.**
Plan for a future South Africa:
- He wants to continue talks but still is in support of the armed struggle, just because this struggle forced the government to begin negotiations after all.
- For similar reasons, Mandela speaks for keeping up sanctions.
- White South Africans should participate in rebuilding the country because they form a necessary part of it and have contributed to shaping the country as it is.
- Apartheid must be overcome, and the whites must be convinced of Mandela's plan for South Africa's future.

Reasons for his attitude:
- In prison, Mandela has come to realize that his true hatred is directed against the system of apartheid, not against the whites themselves.
- He considers this system to be responsible for racial tensions.

5. **Analyse how Mandela's attempts to convince the public "that a new, non-racial South Africa [would] be a better place for all." (l. 26) Focus on how he tries to bridge the gap between blacks and whites by making use of antitheses.**

ANTITHESES	EXPLANATION
– "no contradiction between my continuing support for the armed struggle and my advocating negotiations" (ll. 6 f.) – "out of jail, [...], not yet free" (ll. 12 f.) – "anger towards the whites. But I had none." (ll. 14 f.) – "anger towards white decreased, but my hatred for the system grew." (ll. 15 f.) – "I loved even my enemies while I hated the system" (ll. 16 f.) – "did not want to destroy the country before we freed it" (ll. 19 f.) – "white fears and black hopes" (l. 21)	→ The predominant use of antitheses helps to convey Mandela's message by soothing possible white fears that he is not intending to retaliate, while simultaneously stressing the fact that the system of apartheid must finally be overcome, and that only cooperation between whites and blacks can turn South Africa into a free country. Like this, he attempts to overcome the differences between blacks and whites by pointing at a common goal.

6. **Do further research on Winnie Mandela's vision for a future South Africa. Make sure to include the so-called "Winnie-Mandela necklace", for example. Based on your findings, explain why irreconcilable differences between Nelson and Winnie Mandela eventually led to their separation.**

Während Nelson Mandela nach seiner Haftentlassung eine Politik der Versöhnung anstrebte, repräsentiert Winnie Mandela eher eine Politik der Vergeltung und ist bis heute eine sehr kontroverse Figur in Südafrika, da sie u. a. auch von vielen „Mutter der Nation" genannt wird. Ihre Bodyguards waren für ihr brutales Vorgehen bekannt, besonders schwarzen Südafrikanern gegenüber, die mit dem Apartheid-Regime kollaboriert hatten, und im Jahr 1997 musste Winnie Mandela vor der Truth and Reconciliation Commission (vgl. SB, S. 59) erscheinen, wo sie grober Verstöße gegen die Menschenrechte schuldig gesprochen wurde, z. B. sich einer Form der Lynchjustiz namens Necklacing (oder Halskrausenmethode) bedient zu haben. Dabei wird dem Opfer ein mit Benzin getränkter Autoreifen wie eine Halskette (necklace) um den Hals gelegt und angezündet. Die Verschmelzung von brennendem Gummi mit der Haut führt dazu, dass eine Löschung im Grunde nicht möglich ist. Winnie Mandela sagte im Jahr 1986: „With our boxes of matches and our necklaces we shall liberate this country", was allgemein als Gutheißung des Necklacing gesehen wurde, woraufhin sich der ANC vorübergehend von ihr distanzierte.
Bei der Bewertung der Person Winnie Mandelas und ihrer Politik sollten die Schüler allerdings auch auf persönliche Erfahrungen und Schicksalsschläge hingewiesen werden, z. B. dass Winnie Mandela ein Jahr lang in Einzelhaft gefoltert wurde.
In der Verfilmung von Mandelas Leben aus dem Jahr 2013 (Mandela. Long Walk to Freedom) wird dem sich zuspitzenden Konflikt zwischen Mandela und seiner Frau auch recht viel Raum gewährt.

7. **Write an argument between Nelson and Winnie Mandela in which they justify their views on a future South Africa.**
Individual answer; students should be reminded that the task instruction "justify" requires them to "show adequate grounds for decisions or conclusions", which means that results from tasks 1 to 6 should be taken into consideration.

8. **[...] Based on your knowledge so far, discuss who may lay claim to South Africa's past.** SB p. 52
Individual answer; from the perspective of black South Africans, students could, for example, argue that it is originally their country and that the whites merely came as traders/settlers in the first place, that they had their own culture before the whites came, that their own history was written and taught to them by the whites, etc. From the perspective of white South Africans, the argument might be advanced that they not only colonised the country, but built it up (e. g. infrastructure), that later generations were born in SA and thus can rightfully call it their mother country, etc.

Geschichte an sich ist immer eine Rekonstruktion des Vergangenen, ein Erzählen der Vergangenheit basierend auf geschichtlichen Quellen. Je nach Auswahl und Zusammenstellung der Quellen wird eine bestimmte Denkweise auch begünstigt. Diese Problematik sollte mit den Schülern diskutiert werden. Es empfiehlt sich auch, an dieser Stelle einen Exkurs in die postkoloniale Theorie, z. B. „The Empire Writes Back" (Ashcroft, Griffiths, Tiffin) einzuschieben.

9. **Make a list of the various forms of resistance to apartheid you have come across in chapter 2. Classify them according to a) the degree of publicity, b) the degree of violence involved, and c) the short- and long-term efficiency.**
Individual answer.

Alternativ könnte an dieser Stelle zur Veranschaulichung auch mit dem Stufenmodell des deutschen Historikers Detlev Peukert (1950–1990) gearbeitet werden, das dieser zur Klassifizierung abweichenden Verhaltens im nationalsozialistischen Deutschland entwickelt hatte. Die verschiedenen Formen und Ausprägungen des Widerstandes gegen die Apartheid können an den entsprechenden Stellen im Schaubild eingetragen und in einer Legende erklärt werden, was die folgende Beurteilung der kurz- und langfristigen Wirkung/Effektivität durch die Visualisierung stützen kann.

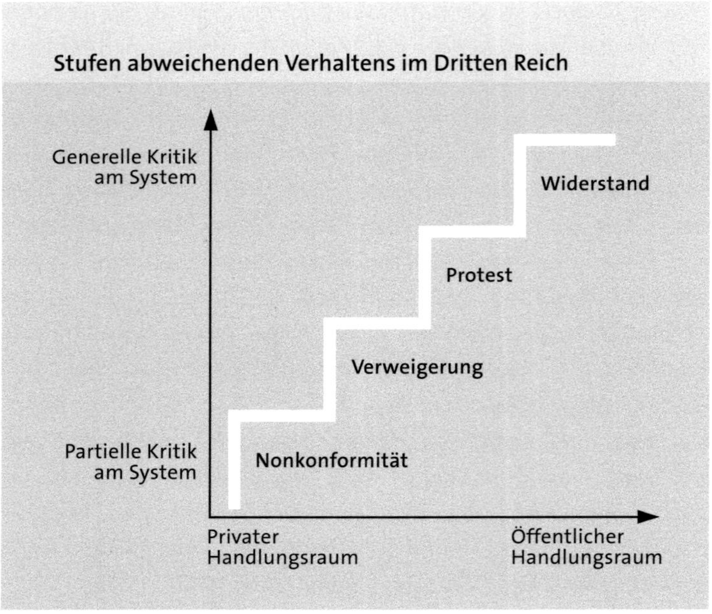

Das Stufenmodell nach Peukert

Language support:

Stufe degree • **abweichendes Verhalten** dissenting behaviour • **Handlungsspielraum** space • **Nonkonformität** non-conformity • **Verweigerung** refusal • **Widerstand** resistance

Model Solution (M 1a, SB p. 21)

3. **Based on your results from tasks 1 and 2, explain if – or to what extent – the shantytown depicted in the picture could possibly be the one described by the narrator in the given excerpt. Give proof from the text to support your standpoint.**

When examining if, or to what extent, the shantytown depicted in the picture accompanying the text could possibly be the one the narrator describes in the excerpt from the novel, one can argue that there are both similarities as well as differences to be detected.

Starting off with the similarities, both picture and novel are set in late 1948, thus on the eve of the official introduction of apartheid. In addition, both feature black people building a township in or in the vicinity of Johannesburg. Another point to be mentioned is that, at least in parts, the construction material one can see in the picture resembles the one mentioned in the text when the narrator speaks of "carry[ing] the iron [...]" (l. 3, cf. also l. 25) The resemblance can be found in the corrugated iron which serves as a door in the dwelling depicted in the photograph.

However, the aspect of the mentioned construction material can also be advanced to argue against the picture showing the shantytown described in the text. The hut-like construction in the picture offers more protection against "[t]he cold wind [that] comes through the sacks" (ll. 27 f.) with which the dwellings are built, according to the narrator, using brick-like stones as their foundation. Another major difference between text and picture is the fact that the narrator frequently mentions that "Shanty Town is up overnight" (ll. 16, 22, 26), the place is soon filled with all kinds of people. Yet, in the picture the area around the house is (still) empty, thus rather giving the impression of an individual "squatter" couple.

In summary, my analysis leads me to the conclusion that the text does not provide sufficient evidence to claim that the picture provided could indeed be the shantytown described by the narrator.

Nobel Prize Acceptance Speech

Desmond Tutu

Listening

1. **True or false? All Russians celebrate the Nobel Peace Prize for Desmond Tutu and have congratulated him.**

☐ True.

☐ False, because ... ______________________________

____

2. **Tutu speaks about the "pall of despondency" (roughly: *Mantel der Niedergeschlagenheit/Mutlosigkeit*) the world has experienced. Tick the experiences he mentions (more than one answer is correct).**

☐ malnourishment ☐ suppression ☐ poverty

☐ famine ☐ insurrections ☐ war

3. **These experiences, says Tutu, have led people to doubt if God cared, if he was**

______________ **and** ______________

and ______________.

4. **According to Tutu, what is the current state of affairs "conclusive proof" of as regards the qualities of God?**

____

____

____

5. **Tutu recalls visiting a friend's house where he saw a book of cartoons entitled "My God". What is Tutu's favourite one? Please quote.**

____

____

6. **Explain the cartoon's message (cf. question 5) against the backdrop of questions 2 to 4.**

____

____

____

7. **Tutu says the prize has given new hope to people who have suffered in South Africa. Tick which examples he gives. More than one answer is correct.**

- ☐ children who have seen their mothers die of starvation in resettlement camps
- ☐ a man who had to live by himself in a single-sex house for months as a consequence of the Pass Laws
- ☐ white students who regret that the education of the black students is inferior
- ☐ human rights activists who have to endure detention in a single cell and torture
- ☐ the ones who were forced to leave their mother country
- ☐ priests who were sentenced to life imprisonment

8. **In short, all those who have new hopes are ____________________,**

oppressed, ____________________, tortured by the powerful tyrants.

9. **True or false? The date the award is made is not important.**

- ☐ True.
- ☐ False, because ... ____________________

____

____

1. **True or false? All Russians celebrate the Nobel Peace Prize for Desmond Tutu and have congratulated him.**
False, because representatives of the Russian Church have congratulated him, but not the Soviet government.

2. **Tutu speaks about the "pall of despondency" (roughly: *Mantel der Niedergeschlagenheit/Mutlosigkeit*) the world has experienced. Tick the experiences he mentions (more than one answer is correct).**
- [ ] malnourishment
- [ ] suppression
- [X] poverty
- [X] famine
- [ ] insurrections
- [X] war

3. **These experiences, says Tutu, have led people to doubt if God cared, if he was omnipotent and loving and compassionate.**

4. **According to Tutu, what is the current state of affairs "conclusive proof" of as regards the qualities of God?**
He says that the world is in such a desolate state that (one could assume that) either God does not exist at all, or, if he exists, that he/she does not care a lot about his/her creation.

5. **Tutu recalls visiting a friend's house where he saw a book of cartoons entitled "My God". What is Tutu's favourite one? Please quote.**
"Oh dear, I think I have lost my copy of the divine plan."

6. **Explain the cartoon's message (cf. question 5) against the backdrop of questions 2 to 4.**
The cartoon seems to take a satirical stand on all the misery the world is afflicted with and suggests that God's "divine plan" for his Creation has turned sour (cf. the suffering Tutu lists, question 2).

7. **Tutu says the prize has given new hope to people who have suffered in South Africa. Tick which examples he gives. More than one answer is correct.**
- [ ] children who have seen their mothers die of starvation in resettlement camps
- [X] a man who had to live by himself in a single-sex house for months as a consequence of the Pass Laws
- [ ] white students who regret that the education of the black students is inferior
- [X] human rights activists who have to endure detention in a single cell and torture
- [X] the ones who were forced to leave their mother country
- [ ] priests who were sentenced to life imprisonment

8. **In short, all those who have new hopes are voiceless, oppressed, dispossessed, tortured by the powerful tyrants.**

9. **True or false? The date the award is made is not important.**
False, because it is 10 December, Human Rights Day. To Tutu, this indicates that there is indeed a God who is benevolent and watches over the people, and so nothing can stop them.

Nobel Prize Acceptance Speech

Desmond Tutu

Your Majesty, your Royal Highness, your Excellency, Mr Chairman, ladies and gentlemen, As I was about to say before we were somewhat interrupted, I would like, first of all, before I give my thanks in acceptance, to say we would like to do this in our African way by singing first. And so I will call on my colleagues from South Africa and my family to join me here whilst we sing.

[*singing & commentary in Norwegian*]

Your Majesty, members of the Royal Family, Mr Chairman, ladies and gentlemen,

Many thousands of people round the world have been thrilled with the award of the Nobel Peace Prize for 1984 to Desmond Mpilo Tutu. I was told of a delegation of American church people who were visiting Russia recently. On hearing the news, they and their hosts ... Russian hosts celebrated the Nobel Peace Prize winner. There has been a tremendous volume of greetings from heads of state, world leaders of the Christian Church and of other faiths as well as from so-called ordinary people – notable exceptions being the Soviet and South African governments.

The prize has given fresh hope to many in a world that has sometimes had a pall of despondency cast over it by the experience of suffering, disease, poverty, famine, hunger, oppression, injustice, evil and war – a pall that has made many wonder whether God cared, whether He was omnipotent, whether He was loving and compassionate. The world is in such desperate straits, in such a horrible mess that it all provides almost conclusive proof that a good and powerful and loving God such as Christians and people of other faiths say they believe in could not exist, or if He did, He really could not be a God who cared much about the fate of His creatures or the world they happened to inhabit which seemed to be so hostile to their aspirations to be fully human.

I once went to a friend's house in England. I found a charming book of cartoons entitled "My God". One showed God with appeals and supplications bombarding Him from people below and God saying, 'I wish I could say, Don't call me, I'll call you.' And another declared 'Create in six days and have eternity to regret it.' My favourite shows God somewhat disconsolate and saying, 'Oh dear, I think I have lost my copy of the divine plan.' Looking at the state of the world you would be forgiven for wondering if He ever had one and whether He had not really botched things up.

New hope has sprung in the breasts of many as a result of this prize – the mother watching her child starve in a Bantustan homeland resettlement camp, or one whose flimsy plastic covering was demolished by the authorities in the KTC squatter camp in Cape Town; the man emasculated by the Pass Laws as he lived for eleven months in a single-sex hostel; the student receiving an inferior education; the activist languishing in a consulate or a solitary confinement cell, being tortured because he thought he was human and wanted that God-given right recognized; the exiled longing to kiss the soil of her much loved motherland, the political prisoner watching the days of a life sentence go by like the drip of a faulty tap, imprisoned because he knew he was created by God not to have his human dignity or pride trodden underfoot.

A new hope has been kindled in the breast of the millions who are voiceless, oppressed, dispossessed, tortured by the powerful tyrants; lacking elementary human rights in Latin America, in South East Asia, in the Far East, in many parts of Africa and behind the Iron Curtain, who have their noses rubbed in the dust. How wonderful, how appropriate that this award is made today – December the 10th, Human Rights Day. It says more eloquently than anything else that this is God's world and He is in charge. That our cause is a just cause, that we will attain human rights in South Africa and everywhere in the world. We shall be free in South Africa and everywhere in the world.

I want to thank the Nobel Committee. I want to thank the churches in Norway and everywhere for their support, their love and their prayers.
On behalf of all these for whom you have given a new hope, a new cause for joy, I want to accept this award in a wholly representative capacity.
I accept this prestigious award on behalf of my family, on behalf of the South African Council of Churches, on behalf of all in my motherland, on behalf of those committed to the cause of justice, of peace, and reconciliation everywhere.
If God be for us, who can be against us? Thank you.
[*singing & commentary in Norwegian*]
(own transcription)

„Auch Jesus war ein Revolutionär"

In issue 43/1984, German magazine DER SPIEGEL conducted an interview with Nobel Peace Prize laureate Bishop Desmond Tutu.

1. Imagine you were spending a school year abroad in South Africa. You find the topic of apartheid very interesting, and you have come across the following interview on the Internet. Prepare a short presentation for your classmates in which you mediate Tutu's statements into English for them.

2. Do further research on Germany's (i. e. the FRG's – Federal Republic of Germany's) reaction(s) to apartheid in order to provide the necessary context for DER SPIEGEL's questions for your classmates.

SPIEGEL: Bischof Tutu, wir möchten Ihnen zum Friedensnobelpreis gratulieren ...

TUTU: Danke schön.

SPIEGEL: Der Präsident Ihres Landes, Pieter Botha*, reagierte lediglich mit einem „No comment" auf Ihre Ehrung. Schmerzt Sie das?

TUTU: Es macht mich traurig. Fremde Regierungen und Staatsoberhäupter haben mich beglückwünscht. Mein eigenes Land aber findet nicht einmal ein konventionelles Wort wie „Wir gratulieren". Das würde doch nicht die Haut auf ihren hohen Nasen ritzen*.

SPIEGEL: Ihre Regierung nennt Sie einen politischen Priester. Stimmt das?

TUTU: Ich glaube, dass ein Christ auch politisch sein muss, wenngleich nicht parteipolitisch*.

SPIEGEL: Sind Sie ein „Priester-Revolutionär", wie Zeitungen Sie nennen?

TUTU: Das Nobelpreiskomitee hat geurteilt, es hat mich und den „South African Council of Churches" (SACC), dessen Generalsekretär ich bin, gerechtfertigt – als Helfer für Versöhnung* und Frieden. Natürlich wollen wir grundlegende Veränderungen. Wenn das Revolution ist, dann bin ich ein Revolutionär. Selbst Jesus war das, er wollte Güte*, Gerechtigkeit und Vergebung*.

SPIEGEL: 1960 hat ein anderer Südafrikaner, Häuptling Albert Luthuli*, Führer des „African National Congress" (ANC), den Friedensnobelpreis bekommen. Als er starb, hieß es, er sei der letzte gemäßigte* schwarze Führer gewesen. Der ANC ging in den Untergrund und versucht seitdem mit Waffengewalt die weiße Herrschaft zu beenden. Vergleichen Sie sich mit Luthuli?

TUTU: Wir wollten beide Südafrika mit friedlichen Mitteln verändern. Er aber war ein Politiker, ich bin ein religiöser Führer.

SPIEGEL: Was Sie sagen, könnte genügen, Sie nach dem Gesetz für innere Sicherheit zu verhaften. Haben Sie nicht manchmal Angst?

TUTU: Nein, nicht wirklich. Ich finde, dass ich nichts sage oder tue, was subversiv* ist. Das gibt natürlich keine Sicherheit, vor allem nicht, wenn man die Handlungen der Regierung während der letzten Jahre verfolgt. Aber Gott ist mein Hirte*.

SPIEGEL: Die Verleihungsschrift* betont, dass nicht nur Sie und der SACC geehrt werden sollen, sondern auch alle Einzelpersonen und Gruppen Südafrikas, die mit „ihrem Bemühen um Menschenwürde*, Brüderlichkeit* und Demokratie die Bewunderung* der Welt haben", nicht zuletzt wegen ihrer friedlichen Methoden. Frage: Wie lange kann der Widerstand friedlich bleiben?

TUTU: Nicht mehr lange. Deswegen habe ich die Weltöffentlichkeit um Hilfe gebeten, um die Regierung Südafrikas an den Konferenztisch zu bringen, bevor es zu spät ist.

SPIEGEL: Was kann die Welt tun, um die Spannung* in Südafrika zu mindern?

TUTU: Sie muss die Zusammenarbeit mit jenen einstellen, welche die Apartheid verursachen.

SPIEGEL: In welchen Bereichen?

Pieter Botha leader of SA from 1978 to 1989, an outspoken opponent of black majority rule

Das ... ritzen. And that wouldn't even scratch the skin on their high noses.
parteipolitisch party-political

Versöhnung conciliation
Güte goodness
Vergebung forgiveness
Luthuli cf. SB, pp. 28 f.

gemäßigt moderate

subversiv subversive (intended to destroy the power or influence of a government or an established belief)
Hirte shepherd
Verleihungsschrift the wording of the award
Menschenwürde human dignity
Brüderlichkeit brotherhood
Bewunderung admiration

Spannung tension

unlängst recently
Glaubwürdigkeit credibility
Richtlinien einhalten to meet requirements
Gewerkschaft trade union
Wanderarbeitersystem roaming-worker system
Passgesetze Pass Laws, cf. SB, p. 32 (annotations)
Abschaffung abolishment
schwere Unruhen violent unrest
geneigt sein to be inclined to do sth.
Warum ... Brotfahrzeuge? Why are children setting fire to houses, wrecking schools and destroying bread vans?
Funken spark
Hendrik Verwoerd Prime Minister of SA from 1958 until his assassination in 1966, often called the "Architect of Apartheid" since he helped to implement the policy as Minister of Native Affairs and later Prime Minister
Endlösung final solution (reference to the so-called "Final Solution to the Jewish Question" the Nazis pursued)
verfrachten to discard

TUTU: Die Großmächte haben oft genug Uno-Aktionen gegen Südafrika durch ihr Veto verhindert. Unlängst* war Botha in Europa und traf dort hohe Regierungsvertreter. Das hat seine Glaubwürdigkeit* gestärkt.

SPIEGEL: Wie denken Sie über ausländische Investitionen in Südafrika?

TUTU: Investitionen sollten nur erlaubt sein, wenn bestimmte Richtlinien eingehalten* werden, zum Beispiel: Schwarze Arbeiter müssen mit ihren Familien in der Nähe ihrer Arbeitsplätze wohnen dürfen. Gewerkschaften* müssen zugelassen sein, und die Investoren sollten versichern, dass sie das Wanderarbeitersystem* und die Passgesetze* für Schwarze ablehnen. Schließlich sollte man der südafrikanischen Regierung 18 bis 24 Monate Zeit geben, diese Bedingungen zu erfüllen.

SPIEGEL: Halten Sie diese Bedingungen in naher Zeit für realisierbar?

TUTU: Nein, das wäre ja die Abschaffung* der Apartheid. Das wäre zu schön.

SPIEGEL: Seit Wochen schon gibt es schwere Unruhen* in Südafrika mit Toten und Verletzten. Vor allem Jugendliche scheinen nicht mehr auf einen fernen Tag warten zu wollen, an dem die Weißen geneigt sind*, über eine Teilung der Macht zu verhandeln. Hat die Revolution schon begonnen?

TUTU: Der Aufstand der Schwarzen begann 1912 mit der Gründung des ANC. Revolution ist nicht nur blutiger Krieg.

SPIEGEL: Sie verstehen Ihre Leute wie sonst kaum jemand: Warum zünden gerade Kinder Häuser an, verwüsten Schulen, vernichten Brotfahrzeuge*?

TUTU: Die Hauptursache jeder Unruhe in Südafrika ist die Apartheid, da genügt ein Funken*. Nehmen Sie nur die schwarze Erziehung. Hendrik Verwoerd*, der Vater der Apartheid, hat ganz klar gesagt, dass Schwarze nicht über ein gewisses Bildungsniveau hinaus erzogen werden sollten, damit sie den Weißen dienen können. Deswegen die Proteste.

SPIEGEL: Kürzlich haben Sie Südafrika mit Nazi-Deutschland verglichen. Ist das nicht, trotz der Apartheid, doch übertrieben?

TUTU: Nein, ich meine die unchristliche Ideologie beider Systeme. In Südafrika ist das Wichtigste am Menschen seine Rasse, wie einstmals in Deutschland. Die Deutschen hatten eine Endlösung*, und diese Typen hier haben auch eine Endlösung. Sie entziehen Menschen ihre Staatsbürgerschaft und werfen sie anschließend weg, indem sie sie in sogenannte Homelands verfrachten*.

SPIEGEL: Falls Präsident Botha sagen würde: „Lassen Sie uns über unsere Probleme reden." Würden Sie hingehen?

TUTU: Ja, aber bei Verhandlungen muss die Themenliste stimmen.

SPIEGEL: Was müsste auf ihr stehen?

TUTU: Das Ende der Apartheid.

o. V., "Auch Jesus war ein Revolutionär", Der Spiegel, Heft 43/1984; www.spiegel.de, 22.10.1984 [10.01.2014]

1. Imagine you were spending a school year abroad in South Africa. You find the topic of apartheid very interesting, and you have come across the given interview on the Internet. Prepare a short presentation for your classmates in which you mediate Tutu's statements into English for them.

Tutu regrets that his own country has not even congratulated him for the award. To the question if he could be called a "priest revolutionary", he answers that he does indeed want fundamental change, and if that was revolutionary, he – like Jesus – can be called such.

Tutu furthermore establishes a parallel between himself and former laureate Luthuli by stating that both of them use(d) peaceful means to achieve their ends, and that he is not afraid of governmental retaliation for his words and deeds, since on the one hand he does not consider himself subversive, and on the other he feels he is protected by God. But he also foreshadows that resistance will not remain non-violent for long, which is why he has asked the world public to participate in making the South African government join talks. This, according to Tutu, could be achieved by ending cooperation with South Africa. He criticizes that the great powers have prevented UN sanctions against South Africa by vetoing them, and that Botha's meetings with state representatives during his travels to Europe have enhanced his credibility. As regards foreign investments in South Africa, Tutu does not reject those completely, but wants certain requirements to be met, such as the foundation of trade unions or the abolishment of the Pass Laws. However, he concedes that these requirements are rather unrealistic at the moment since they would in effect mean the abolishment of apartheid. Asked about recent violent unrests in South Africa, Tutu claims the revolution began with the foundation of the ANC in 1912 and rejects the notion that a revolution by necessity must be violent. Apartheid, says Tutu, is the main reason for any unrest in South Africa by, for example, making sure that the education of black South Africans does not exceed a certain level in order to deem them proper servants for the whites.

He maintains that the non-Christian ideologies of Nazi Germany and South Africa are comparable, since both attach utmost important to the concept of "race" and both aim at a "final solution" which in South Africa consists of withdrawing the people's citizenship and discarding them into so-called "homelands", says Tutu.

Yet he would be willing to participate in talks with South Africa's government, but only in case the end of apartheid is on the agenda.

2. Do further research on Germany's reaction(s) to apartheid in order to provide the necessary context for DER SPIEGEL's questions for your classmates.

Die BRD kooperierte mit Südafrika und unterstützte den Apartheid-Staat militärisch und wirtschaftlich, was vor allem durch die deutsche Anti-Apartheid-Bewegung (gegr. 1974) in den 70er-Jahren aufgedeckt wurde. Die BRD verstieß damit gegen das völkerrechtlich verbindende Rüstungs-Embargo der UNO gegen Südafrika, das 1977 ausgesprochen wurde (vgl. M 3, Aufg. 5). Die 1948 verabschiedete Menschenrechts-Erklärung der UNO (vgl. M 4, Aufg. 4) wurde durch den „Ausbruch" des Kalten Krieges praktisch außer Kraft gesetzt, und Südafrika war für den sogenannten „freien Westen" nicht nur aufgrund seiner geografischen Lage von strategischer Bedeutung, sondern auch wegen seiner Mineralvorkommen, hier besonders Uran (→ nukleare Aufrüstung). Vor diesem Hintergrund erscheinen einige Fragen der SPIEGEL-Reporter fast zynisch, wie zum Beispiel die Frage nach Tutus Haltung ausländischen Investitionen gegenüber (vgl. Z. 51).

Weitere Informationen zur deutschen Anti-Apartheid-Bewegung und der Kooperation der BRD mit den südafrikanischen Apartheid-Regimes finden sich unter: www.friedenskooperative.de/ff/ff05/7-71.htm.

In seinem Roman „The Girl Who Saved the King of Sweden" (vgl. M 9a) greift Jonas Jonasson das Thema des angeblichen Atombomben-Besitzes Südafrikas humoristisch auf.

No Time Like the Present

Nadine Gordimer

Nobel Prize-winning Nadine Gordimer's last published novel during her lifetime (1923 – 2014), *No Time Like the Present*, illustrates the crisis of identity in post-apartheid South Africa. The novel begins with the following excerpt, a brief review of the life of Jabu and Steve, a mixed couple, under the pressures of racial segregation and injustice.

1. Before reading, brainstorm in class: What do you already know about the time from when apartheid was officially introduced to when it was abolished?
2. Do some research on South Africa's Immorality Act. Present your findings in a mind map or in any other form of visualization.
3. "There's no time like the present" is a well-known saying. Look up its meaning in a dictionary and think about a possible link between this saying and the story told in Gordimer's book.
4. **Present** the couple introduced in the excerpt, their living conditions and their family background.
5. **Analyse** by which means the novelist introduces the couple. Focus on narrative perspective as well as syntax and stylistic devices.
6. Based on the narrator's view on identity, **discuss** what further component elements determine a person's identity. (A mind map may help you to structure your thoughts before writing them down.)

Glengrove Place. It isn't a glen* and there isn't a grove*. It must have been named by a Scot or Englishman for features of a home left behind, when he made money in this city at more than five thousand feet* and entered the property market enterprise.

But it has been a place. It was somewhere they could live – together, when there wasn't anywhere to do so lawfully. The rent for the apartment was high, for them then, but it included a certain complicity* on the part of the owner of the building and the caretaker, nothing comes for nothing when law-abiding* people are taking some risk of breaking the law. As a tenant*, he had the kind of English- or European-sounding name no different from others usual on the tenants' mailboxes beside the elevator in the entrance; a potted cactus decorative there, if there was no grove. She was simply the added appendage* 'Mrs'. They actually *were* married, although that was unlawful, too. In the neighbouring country where she had gone into exile just over the border to study, and he, a young white man whose political affiliations* made it necessary for him to disappear from the university in the city for a time, they, imprudently ignoring the consequence inevitable back home, had fallen in love and got themselves married.

Back home in South Africa, she became a teacher at a private school run by the Fathers of a Catholic order tolerated outside state-segregated education, able there to use her natural surname on non-racial principles.

She was black, he was white. That was all that mattered. All that was identity then. Simple as the black letters on this white page. It was in those two identities that they transgressed*. And got away with it, more rather than less. They were not visible enough, politically well known enough to be worth prosecution* under the Immorality Act*, better to be watched, followed if they might, on the one hand, make footprints which could lead to more important activists, or on the chance they might be candidates for recruitment to report back from whatever level, dissident to revolutionary, they were privy to*. [...]

glen a deep narrow valley in Scotland or Ireland
grove a piece of land with trees growing on it
city at more than five thousand feet Johannesburg, which is one of South Africa's higher cities
complicity involvement in a situation, especially one that is morally wrong
law-abiding respectful of the law and obeying it
tenant sb. who lives in a house, room etc. and pays rent to the person who owns it
appendage sth. that is connected to a larger or more important thing
affiliation the involvement that sb. has with a political, religious etc. organization
to transgress *formal* to do something that is against the rules of social behaviour or against a moral principle
prosecution when a charge is made against sb. for a crime
Immorality Act reference to the 2nd Immorality Act of 1957 that continued prohibiting interracial sex and marriage
to be privy to sth. sharing in the knowledge of facts that are secret

She was black, but there's a great deal more to that now than what was the beginning and end of existence as recorded in an outdated file of an outdated country, even though the name hasn't changed. She was born black in that time; her name is a signature to the past from which she comes, christened in the Methodist church where one of her grandfathers had been a pastor and her father, headmaster at a local school for black boys, was an Elder, her mother chairlady of the church ladies' society. The Bible was the source of baptismal first names along with the second, African ones, with which white people, whom the child would grow up to have to please, deal with in this world, had no association of identity. Rebecca Jabulile.

He was white. But that's also not as definitive as coded in old files. Born in the same past era, a few years before her, he's a white mix – that was of no significance so long as the elements were white. Actually, his mix is quite complicated in certain terms of identity not determined by colour. His father was a gentile*, secular, nominally* observant Christian, his mother Jewish. It is the mother's identity which is decisive in the identity of a Jew, the mother whom one can be sure of when it comes to parental conception. If the mother is Jewish that is the claim for her son within the faith, and of course this implies ritual circumcision*. His father evidently raised no objection, perhaps like many agnostics* even atheists he secretly envied those practising the illusion of a religious faith – or was it indulgence* for the wife he loved. If that's what she wanted, important to her in a way he didn't understand. Let the foreskin be cut.

Nadine Gordimer, No Time Like the Present, Bloomsbury Publishing Plc., London 2013, pp. 1–3, first published in 2012

gentile sb. who is not Jewish
nominally only officially but not really true
circumcision the act of cutting off the skin at the end of the penis as part of a religious ceremony
agnostic sb. who believes that people cannot know whether God exists or not
indulgence the act of allowing sb. else to have whatever they want

1. Before reading, brainstorm in class: What do you already know about the time from when apartheid was officially introduced to when it was abolished?
Individual answers.

2. Do some research on South Africa's Immorality Act. Present your findings in a mind map or in any other form of visualization.
Example:

1st Immorality Act (1927)
- prohibited sexual intercourse outside of marriage between black and white people
- penalty up to 5 years imprisonment for men, 4 years for women
- amendment extended the prohibition to intercourse between white and coloured or Asian people
- 2nd Immorality Act (1957), renamed Sexual Offences Act
- prohibited sexual intercourse and immoral or indecent acts between white and nonwhite people
- penalty up to 7 years for both partners
- amendment increased the number of offences

3. "There's no time like the present" is a well-known saying. Look up its meaning in a dictionary and think about a possible link between this saying and the story told in Gordimer's book.
"There's no time like the present" is said to encourage someone to take action immediately instead of waiting.
To the characters of Gordimer's novel it means that, in view of the growing gap between affluence and mass poverty in post-apartheid South Africa, there can be no freedom from personal involvement. Willing to tackle and remedy the deplorable situation, Jabu and Steve are staying in Johannesburg instead of immigrating to Australia with their children.

4. Present the couple introduced in the excerpt, their living conditions and their family background.

SHE	HE
Rebecca Jabulile	unnamed
black	white
practising Methodist	non-practising Jew (circumcised)
studied in the neighbouring country (Swaziland)	studied at the university of Johannesburg
became a teacher at a private Catholic school	unmentioned

LIVING CONDITIONS	
clandestine lovers under racist law	
got married illegally	
political activists against South African apartheid	
forced to live in exile before returning to Johannesburg	
have to hide their living together in a white part of town	
dependent on the good will and confidentiality of landlord, caretaker, etc.	
FAMILY BACKGROUND	
a pastor among her grandfathers	grandparents unmentioned
her father is an Elder and headmaster of a local school for boys	his father is a non-practising Christian, or rather an agnostic
her mother is chairlady of the church ladies' society	his mother is a practising Jew; traditionally, her faith is also that of her children

5. **Analyse by which means the novelist introduces the couple. Focus on narrative perspective as well as syntax and stylistic devices.**

NARRATIVE PERSPECTIVE:

The omniscient narrator introduces the two main characters in a predominantly depersonalized voice. Throughout the excerpt, he leaves no doubt that he knows everything about the couple: about their families, their education, their political involvement, the trouble living together in a country divided into black and white, etc. Chronicling the couple's life during apartheid, he uses the 3rd-person pronouns "they" (e.g. ll. 4, 11, 14, 21 ff.), "he", "him" (e.g. ll. 8, 13, 19, 38 ff.) and "she", "her" (e.g. ll. 10, 12, 19, 26 ff.). Only the female character's first names, Rebecca Jabulile, are mentioned towards the end of the excerpt, whereas her husband remains unnamed. But, like all omniscient narrators, he also offers commentary that reveals his attitude toward the characters and the events he is telling the reader about: he starts by explaining the street name "Glengrove Place" and what it meant to the couple to have a place of their own; he criticises their careless dealing with imminent threats (cf. ll. 14/15, criticism expressed through his choice of words: "imprudently", "ignoring", "inevitable"), comments on the injustice of apartheid (e.g. ll. 21–28, 28 ff.) and on circumcision as a religious initiation ritual (cf. ll. 42–45).

Actually, what we hear may easily be mistaken for the voice of the novelist herself trying to hide in a narrator.

SYNTAX:

Gordimer's prose has often been criticised as "gnarled and knotty" (Boyd Tonkin, *The Independent*, 16/03/12); it certainly is idiosyncratic. What may be responsible for its occasional opaqueness is mainly syntax: sentences are constructed irregularly or fractured by means of interpolated subordinate clauses, some are even grammatically incorrect, thus hard to understand. Very long and convoluted sentences take turns with short sentences and ellipses (e.g. ll. 1, 4, 11, 21–25, 35). The latter usually contain the more important information, stressed by sudden halts and repetition (e.g. ll. 20/21, 28, 37). Overly obvious antithetical structuring ("he" v. "she", "lawful" v. "unlawful", "white" v. "black", "exile" v. "home", "somewhere" v. "anywhere", etc.) emphasises the didactic intention of the text.

STYLISTIC DEVICES:

Apart from the abundant use of contrast and repetition, there is figurative language: Jabu, whose name must not appear on the mailbox, is metaphorically called an "appendage" (l. 10); the mixed couple's identity is graphically compared to "black letters on this white page" (l. 20). More important activists than Jabu and Steve leave "footprints" (l. 23), Steve's identity as a white man is said to be "not as definitive as coded

in old files" (l. 35), which is one more simile. The last sentence, "Let the foreskin be cut", an ironical statement, supplies one of Gordimer's running motifs: circumcision as a symbol of unhealed scars.
Last but not least, it is worth mentioning that the term "identity" occurs six times in this excerpt, a clear clue to the problem it centres on.

6. **Based on the narrator's view on identity, discuss what further component elements determine a person's identity. (A mind map may help you to structure your thoughts before writing them down.)**
According to the narrator, race alone defined a person's identity in apartheid South Africa (cf. ll. 21/22), whereas for a white person other criteria such as naming (cf. ll. 8/9) and religion (cf. l. 38 ff.) may also have been relevant.
Individual answer, for example:

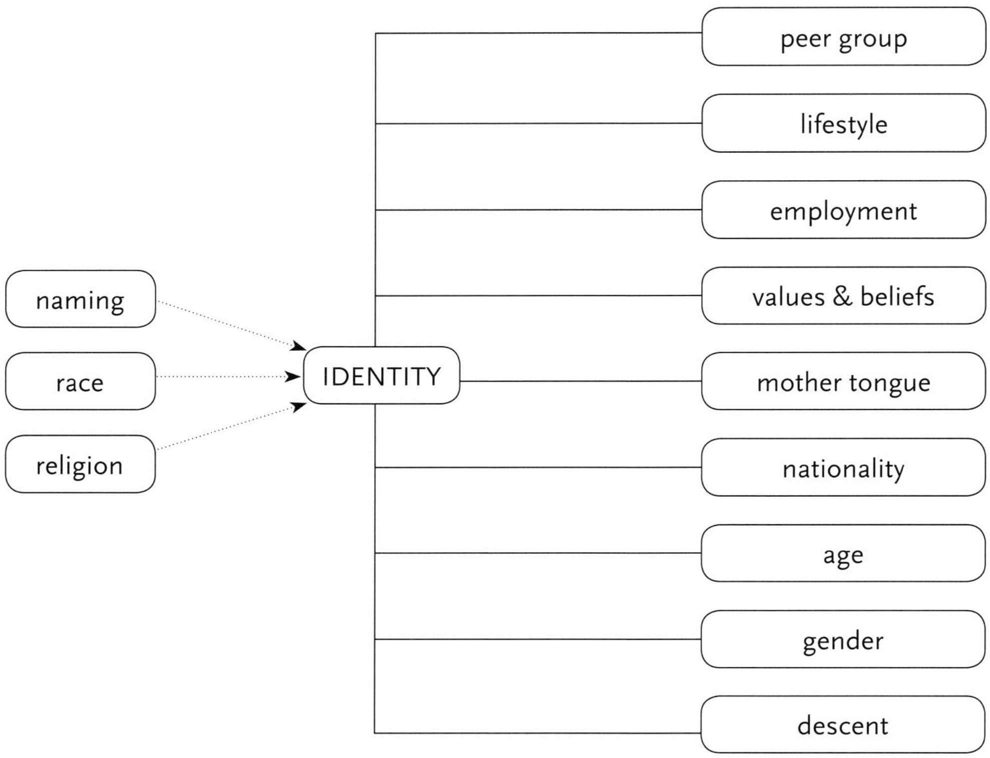

Additional material
@ SNG-40657-013
see Webcode

Nadine Gordimer: No Time Like the Present

Crossword

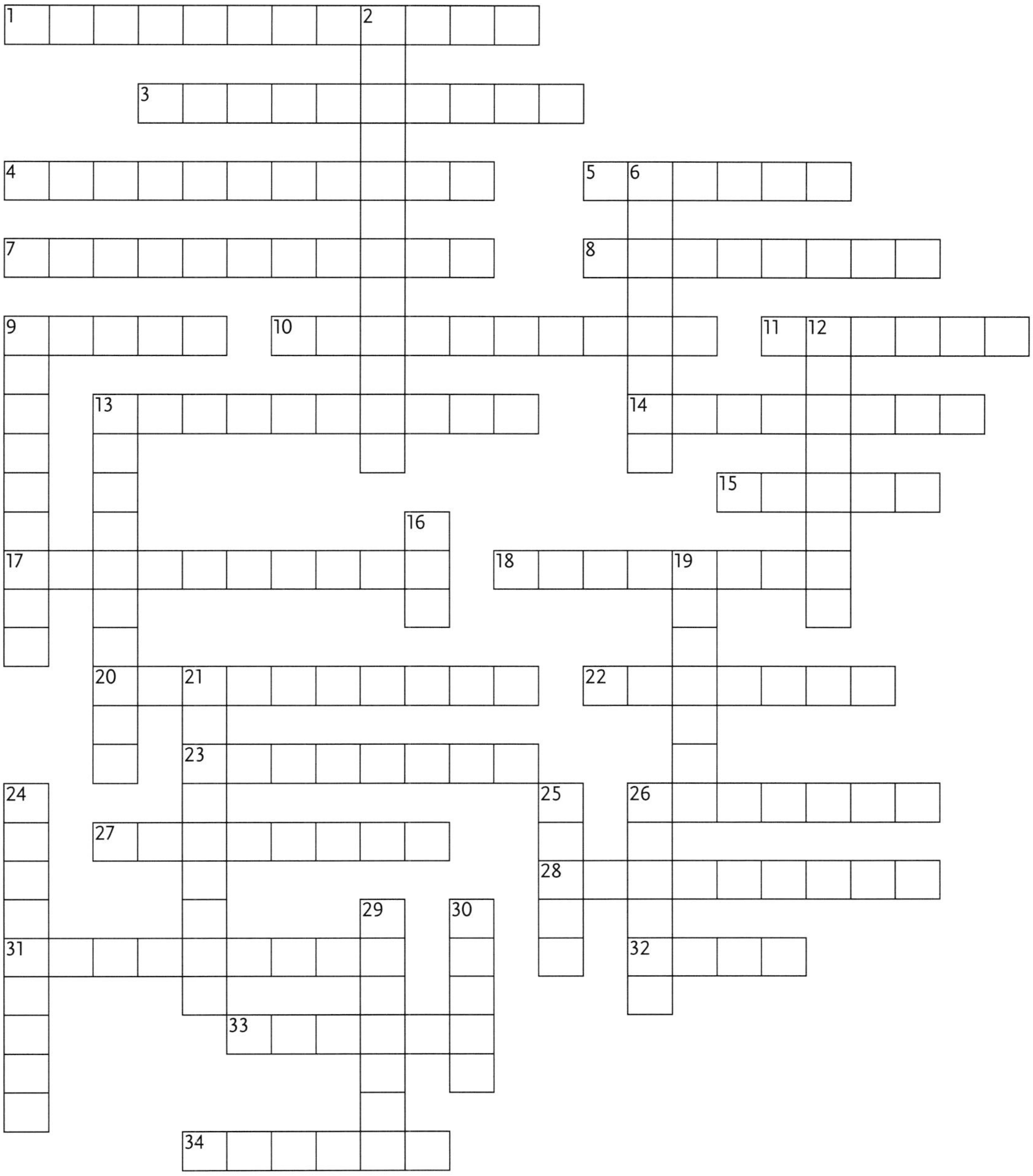

Across:

1 cutting of the skin at the penis tip in a religious ceremony
3 opposite of 'integrated'
4 when a charge is made against sb. for a crime
5 adjective relating to 'race'
7 sb's involvement with a political organization
8 synonym for 'illegal'
9 synonym for 'religion'
10 do sth. against a moral principle
11 official line that separates two countries
13 involvement in a morally wrong situation
14 qualities that make sb. different from other people
15 rights that belong to you
17 synonym for 'unavoidable'
18 adjective related to 'decision'
20 allowing sb. else to have whatever they want
22 sb. who is not Jewish
23 allow people to do, say or believe sth. without criticizing them
26 persuade sb. to do sth. for you
27 synonym for 'baptize'
28 synonym for 'careless'
31 sth. that is connected to a more important thing
32 possibility that sth. bad or dangerous may happen
33 ceremony that is always performed in the same way
34 behave as if you had not heard or seen sth.

Down:

2 synonym for 'meaning'
6 sb. who believes that people cannot know whether God exists or not
9 marked effect or impression
12 synonym for 'old-fashioned'
13 process by which a woman becomes pregnant
16 sb. whose religion is Judaism
19 name that you share with your parents or husband/wife
21 directly influence or decide sth.
24 sth. that is closely related to a person
25 obey a decision, rule or agreement
26 give information about other people to the police or sb. in authority
29 not connected with a church or other religious authority
30 situation in which you are forced to leave your country and live in another one

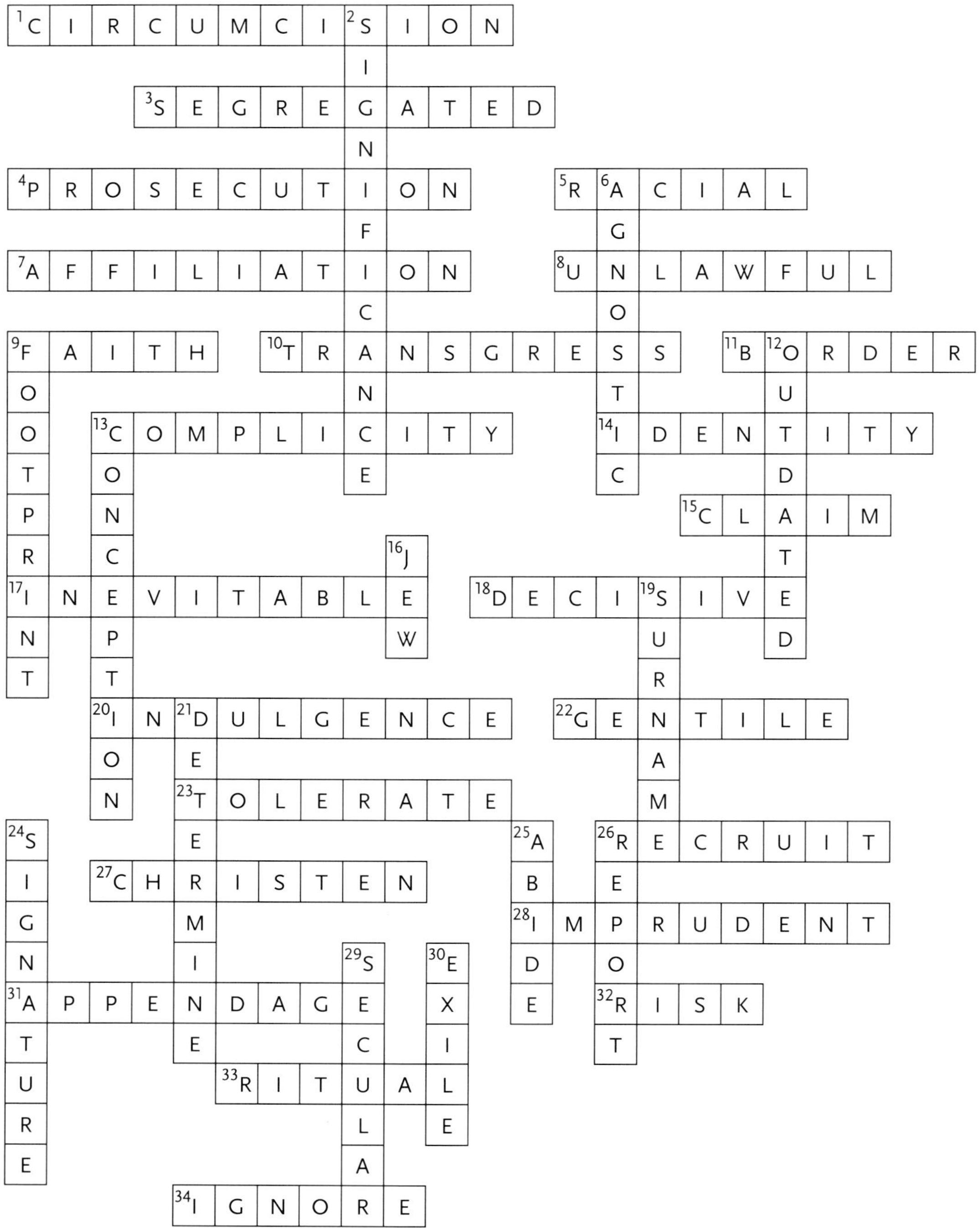
1 CIRCUMCISION
2 SIGNIFICANCE
3 SEGREGATED
4 PROSECUTION
5 RACIAL
6 AGNOSTIC
7 AFFILIATION
8 UNLAWFUL
9 FAITH
9 FOOTPRINT
10 TRANSGRESS
11 BORDER
12 OUTDATED
13 COMPLICITY
13 CONCEPTION
14 IDENTITY
15 CLAIM
16 JEW
17 INEVITABLE
18 DECISIVE
19 SURNAME
20 INDULGENCE
21 DETERMINE
22 GENTILE
23 TOLERATE
24 SIGNATURE
25 ABIDE
26 RECRUIT
26 REPORT
27 CHRISTEN
28 IMPRUDENT
29 SECULAR
30 EXILE
31 APPENDAGE
32 RISK
33 RITUAL
34 IGNORE

Mandela's Rule: Turning Wrong into Right?

M1 Mandela's Bust

SB p. 53

1. **Compare Mandela's bust with the first footage of Mandela and his wife Winnie after his release (cf. chapter 2, p. 51). What is the artwork reflecting?**
Individual answers; students might not know that during his imprisonment (more than 27 years) Mandela was largely unseen and unheard. The artwork shows a strong man with a determined expression. This reflects that people were expecting or hoping for a change in South Africa.
Compared to the footage of Mandela and Winnie, it is obvious that Mandela aged and does not look as young as expected.
The TIME magazine cover from February 1990 serves even better to make students understand that nobody knew what Mandela looked like (see Webcode).

SNG-40657-014 @

M2 The Child Is Not Dead

Ingrid Jonker

SB p. 53

1. **Look at the title and the occasion at which the poem was presented. What do you expect?**
Individual answers.

2. **Outline the structure and topic(s) of the poem.**
Structure: The poem comprises four stanzas. Three of the four stanzas have five lines and the last stanza has eight lines. Depending on the English translation of this poem, some versions have four stanzas of five lines and end with a triplet.
The poem grows in length from the beginning to the end; the last line ends abruptly and unexpectedly.
Topic: Memory of those who died will live on; the repercussions of their lives will live on and nobody is insignificant.

3. **Analyse how the poem illustrates the history of the nation. Focus on language.**
History of a nation: Nyanga was a centre of protest against the Pass Laws in March 1960 and Jonker was deeply moved by the report of a child who was with his mother on the way to a doctor and who was shot by the police.
Language:
   - The poem works with **oppositions** and **enumerations**: the first lines of every stanza contradict the title that suggests the child is dead, but the stanzas repeat in l. 2 and l. 12 that the child is not dead and in l. 3 and l. 7 the child raises its fists, etc.
   - There is **no rhyming pattern** but a clear purpose to the line length.
   - Another opposition is that the child remains silent but "the mother screams", "the father screams" and there are shootings.
   - Jonker makes use of **alliterations and parallelisms**: "police station in Philippi", "the child raises its fists against his mother" and "the child raises his fists against his father".

4. **A publishing house is planning an issue with an anthology dealing with literature in post-apartheid. Evaluate if Jonker's poem is a good contribution to this anthology. Please refer to the poem in your evaluation.**

Ingrid Jonker (19 September 1933–19 July 1965) was a South African poet. Although she wrote in Afrikaans, her poems have been widely translated into other languages. Jonker has reached iconic status in South Africa and is often called the South African Sylvia Plath, owing to the intensity of her work and the tragic course of her turbulent life. She famously was estranged to her father due to her anti-apartheid leanings.
As the post-apartheid government has become more Africanist, the contribution of not only Afrikaners but other minority groups to the liberation struggle has been devalued.
The role of Afrikaans writers needs to be adequately recognized. A narrative of a country, a writing from the Cape, shows that histories are intertwined when using a poem by an Afrikaans woman from the 1960s.

5. **Justify Mandela's use of a poem originally written in Afrikaans by a white South African poet before such an important speech.**

The Mandela government promoted a policy of reconciliation. By reading this note he wanted all South Africans to take note of Jonker's humanity, hoping that they would embrace the policy of reconciliation.
Moreover, according to Mandela we owe to Ingrid Jonker a debt to life itself and also a commitment to the poor, wretched, and despised. All in all, Mandela chose this poem as he believed it helps to discourage ignorance and promote change.
Last, Ingrid Jonker, rather than enjoying her privileged life as a white, voiced her strong opposition against the government's apartheid policies through poetry.

M3 Inauguration Speech, 9 May 1994

Nelson Mandela

SB p. 54

1. **Outline Mandela's main ideas put forward in his speech.**

The speech at hand is a symbolic speech that speaks of humanity and racial reconciliation and recognizes the importance of the turning point in South Africa, indicative of change and transition from apartheid to democracy.
<u>Main ideas:</u>

- A new beginning for South Africa where everyone is a citizen no matter to which ethnicity he or she belongs
- Indicative of change: Cape of Good Hope, where the history has started, serves as the place for the new beginning and spirit of hope
- Mandela envisions a fight for democracy where everyone participates and speaks inclusively
- Transition from apartheid to democracy, emerging from conflicts of the past
- He concludes the speech with plans for the future: reform, reconciliation and unity
- Unity is the underlying theme of Mandela's inaugural address as well as his presidency: the unity of white and black people; the dissolution of apartheid and its associated segregation; the reunification of native South Africans with their homeland

2. **Examine how Mandela's speech has a reconciliatory spirit, focusing on argumentative structure and stylistic devices. To what extent is the photo on p. 55 supporting Mandela's speech?**

Argumentative structure:
- ll. 1–14: introduction – outline/description of the situation in which the population of South Africa finds itself
- ll. 15–25: remedies to solve the situation that is intended to be preserved by the whites
- ll. 26–40: establishes the contrast between white attitudes and black demands
- ll. 41–53: specifies the black population's demands and desires as the only remedy to the current grievances
- ll. 54–61: political equality as the cornerstone of change, even though feared by the white minority
- ll. 62–66: personal conclusion – ideals described before are worth living and dying for
- ll. 67–80: call to action, and problems and issues that are addressed
- ll. 81–92: concludes with plans for the future; plans for change, reform, reconciliation, unity and, most importantly, freedom

Stylistic devices, e. g.:
- **Use of personal pronouns** (we, our) to embody a sense of collectivity: l. 67 "it requires us all to work together"; "our diversity" (l. 68) "we are [...] fully committed to the spirit of a government of national unity" (ll. 85–86); "we will all rise" (l. 92).
- Employing **ideographs** like "liberty", "justice", and "peace" to show the principles of the new political culture in South Africa which includes all citizens regardless of colour.
- The rhetorical style most prevalent in this speech is **pathos**: Mandela begins the speech by acknowledging the national victory, as well as the victory of his presidential campaign, (ethos) and rejoices with his fellow South Africans, giving them a sense of assurance, pride, and hope.
- Mandela then refers to the nation's troublesome past to remind them of the "epic wars of resistance" they endured, using detailed terms like "dungeon" and "dragged in chains" to signify the darkness they have emerged from and the struggles they have overcome.
- **Use of keywords:** He appeals to race and place in ll. 10–30: the claim on land can be thought of as an identification of race with place; for instance, Robben Island where black fighters have been imprisoned.
- **Use of appeal and a strong command:** "it needs action" (l. 67); "They want change!" (l. 69).

Photo: When Nelson Mandela was joyfully inaugurated as South Africa's new president, he seized F. W. de Klerk by the hand and they raised their palms in a joint display of triumph, showing that this would lead to the creation of a "New South Africa". Furthermore this significant occasion illustrates that these two men had just accomplished a political miracle, transforming South Africa into a democracy without a civil war.

3. Discuss if this speech is addressing all people in South Africa and refer to examples from the text.

As mentioned above, the speech is meant to reconcile and Mandela addresses all people in South Africa, regardless of gender, colour, etc., which can be seen in the following lines:
- ll. 1–4: "we are entering a new era for our country and its people. Today we celebrate not the victory of a party, but a party for all the people of South Africa."
- ll. 10–14: "The South Africa we have struggled for, in which all our people, be they African, Coloured, Indian or White, regard themselves as citizens of one nation is at hand."

- ll. 35–40: "The struggle for democracy has never been a matter pursued by one race, class, religious community or gender among South Africans. In honouring those who fought to see this day arrive, we honour the best sons and daughters of all our people. We can count amongst them Africans, Coloureds, Whites, Indians, Muslims, Christians, Hindus, Jews – all of them united by a common vision of a better life for the people of this country."

M4 Country of My Skull

Antjie Krog

SB p. 57

1. Inform yourself about the main idea of the *Truth and Reconciliation Commission* and *Ubuntu*, the African idea of shared humanity.

Truth and Reconciliation Commission (TRC): was a restorative justice body assembled in South Africa after the abolition of apartheid.
Victims and witnesses were invited to give witness of their experiences of rights violations during apartheid. Perpetrators of violence could also give testimony and request amnesty from both civil and criminal prosecution.
The main idea of the TRC was to record the horrible human rights violations and, furthermore, to offer another way of rehabilitation and reparation.
It is an experiment in the healing of a nation as apartheid dehumanised black people.
Ubuntu: an ethical concept that can be translated with "human kindness" and a philosophy that calls on us to mirror our humanity for each other. The philosophy of Ubuntu is derived from the Nguni word, *ubuntu*, meaning "the quality of being human." Ubuntu manifests itself through various human acts, clearly visible in social, political, and economic situations, as well as among family. This idea seems to have resonated with some of the victims who gave evidence, like Cynthia Ngewu, mother of Christopher Piet, one of the Gugulethu Seven: "This thing called reconciliation ... if I am understanding it correctly it means this perpetrator, this man who has killed [my son], if it means he becomes human again, this man, so that I, so that all of us get our humanity back ... then I agree, then I support it all."

2. Try to guess why Krog might have titled her book *Country of My Skull*.

Individual answers; Krog has sliced beneath the skin of her country and this might be a reason why she calls it "Country of My Skull"; she is exposing a South Africa and its past that outsiders do not know.
The title alludes to interconnectedness between the author and her country, the country of her skull.

3. Krog is making use of different genres of texts in the excerpt at hand. Sum up the first hearing and then outline the structure of the excerpt.

Summary:

- The given excerpt from *Country of My Skull* opens with the beginning of the hearings of the TRC in April 1994.
- First, the setting of the commission is described and then the fears of Archbishop Tutu, who is one of the Commissioners.
- The hearings open with the Xhosa hymn and a prayer by Tutu.
- After greeting the victims, the activities of the reporting journalists, who are broadcasting live, are described.

Structure:
First, the given excerpt seems to be an article for a newspaper (cf. ll. 1–5) and then it seems to be a narrative. In line 33 the narrative stops and "To seize the surge of lan-

guage by its soft, bare skull" (l. 34) looks like a reflection of Krog or at least a caesura, followed by a monologue or a new narrative thread (cf. ll. 35–37). Then the testimonies in the TRC hearings follow (cf. ll. 38–67).

→ A text that transgresses the boundaries between fact and fiction

4. **Analyse how Krog's use of fiction, fact and language makes an impact on the reader.**

Use of fictional and factual language:

- Krog is transposing the testimonies and non-fictional texts into a fictional narrative and tries to mold a new literate medium to deal with what she perceives during the TRC hearings.
- She is "quilting" (quote by Krog) her text to create a multi-vocal text in order to illustrate that there is no coherent nation or truth to the hearings. In the given excerpt it is not clear whether the testimonies were given at the TRC or whether the textual material was used.
- "To seize the surge of language by its soft, bare skull" (l. 34) might indicate that the narrator is not sure how many layers of skin, and thus identity, she has as she speaks about language, which is a marker of social identity.

Use of language:

Krog uses dashes, ellipses and inserts dots/apostrophes to suggest a wide range of voices and narrates the testimonies from the point of view of the witnesses or bereaved.

→ The gap between original and interpreted text remains unclear and illustrates that the narrator is torn.

→ Thus, the reader gets mingled and wrapped around the painful stories and testimonies during the TRC hearings.

5. **Compare the two different book covers and decide which you would choose if you were the person who is in charge.**

Individual answer;

- The first cover shows Joyce Mtimkulu, the mother of a victim. During the Truth and Reconciliation Commission she is holding all that is left of her son. This cover illustrates a more personal level of the TRC and shows a photo of the bereaved.
- The South African edition shows a South African landscape, with no human presence. Disembodied landscapes or empty spaces are associated with Afrikaans literature and one assumption is that Krog's *Country of My Skull* is meant to address white South Africans or even the fact that disembodied landscapes do not include indigenous South Africans, as the title is *Country of My Skull*.

6. **Discuss if reconciliation is possible without any jurisdiction against the backdrop of the atrocities during apartheid.**

In favour of TRC and the concept:

✓ For a successful reconciliation the bereaved and the victims have to accept that the gross violations and atrocities of criminals will not be unpunished.

✓ Jurisdiction does not mean fairness: some cases are time-barred, so there is no jurisdiction possible; in a trial the perpetrator might be charged and sentenced but the victim cannot discuss the consequences of the crime/offence.

✓ Another advantage of the TRC is that it empowers them to address issues and concerns surrounding the crime and its consequences.

✓ The TRC can be compared to the concept of the victim – offender mediation:

- ➢ providing the parties with a process which can lead to new insight, thereby reducing levels of anxiety, and contributing to therapeutic gains
- ➢ addressing questions and concerns regarding the offender's eventual release into the community

➢ providing sensitive staff who are committed to being agents of healing and restoration for those who suffer crime's effects.

➔ A way for a society to move forward and not dwell in the past

➔ A good way to deal with human rights abuses if a democratic government replaces a repressive government

Against the TRC and the concept:

✓ Some of the offences are unspeakable and it might be difficult to face the deeds of the perpetrators, especially when the perpetrators are not repentant.

✓ Many apartheid victims believe that the process has failed because amnesties were granted to the perpetrators and no reparations were made or paid.

✓ Violators of human rights might believe that they get away without punishment.
  ➔ Amnesty at the expense of justice does not promote reconciliation

Wenn Sie das Thema TRC vertiefen möchten, eignen sich hier einige Filme: u. a. In my Country (2004), Long Night's Journey into Day (2000) und Red Dust (2004).

M 5 Sports and Politics

SB p. 60

1. Compare the photos of the Springboks in 1956, 2000 and 2007 (M 5a). What is striking?

Noticeably, in 1956 there is no black rugby player in South Africa's rugby team. This is due to the introduction of apartheid in 1948, the Population Registration Act in 1950 and the Bantu Homelands Act in 1951 (cf. pp. 7–8, Getting started & timeline). But even before the apartheid laws were implemented, many nations and teams excluded non-white players or left them at home when they toured in South Africa. For instance, New Zealand left all players of Maori origin at home.
After the Sharpeville massacre, criticism against South Africa and the Springboks started and the Springboks became a symbol of racial division.

2. Make an educated guess why the last photo with Mandela handing the Rugby World Cup to the captain of the Springboks in an iconic image of sports and politics combined.

As mentioned before, the Springboks had been the personification of apartheid. Wearing a Springbok shirt and handing the World Cup to Pienaar, the captain of the Springboks and a white Afrikaner, is a gesture of reconciliation and another step towards the idea of "The Rainbow Nation" coined by D. Tutu.
Mandela understood the unifying character of sports and supported the team from the beginning of the World Cup which was hosted and then won by South Africa in 1995. So, the victory of the Springboks served as a symbol of a united country.

3. Skim the transcript and point out the meaning of rugby after apartheid.

Even after apartheid, rugby is not a unifying sports event: all blacks are cheering for another team, to be precise for England and not for South Africa.
Mandela realises the power of sport events and tries to support the Springboks and unite his country.
All in all, at the very beginning of the 1995 World Cup, rugby was still a symbol and embodiment of apartheid.

4. Now, watch the trailer for *Invictus* online and examine by which means rugby is shown as a unifying symbol in South Africa. Focus on cinematic devices and music.

Cinematic devices:

✓ Stills: The trailer makes use of **dissolves** (when two shots overlap) and fades several times into black (**transition**).

→ These devices show, as the terms indicate, a transition into a unified country and therefore the dissolving of the old prejudices within South African society.

✓ COLOURS: Employed to show the racial division. For example, the first screen shot shows white boys dressed in neat, white sweatshirts, playing rugby. Separated from the Afrikaans boys, we see on the other side of a fence ragged black kids dressed in insignificant colours, playing football.
→ Forthright image of a divided society in 1990

✓ CAMERA MOVEMENTS: For example stills no. 4 and 1 use a tracking shot, first to indicate the separation between black and white and to establish the context of the separation. In still number 4, the hand-held camera is used to underline the steady movement of rugby.
Still no. 5 is a medium shot; the captain of the team and Chester Williams, the only black rugby player in the team, are shown side by side and on the same eye-level.
→ Used to illustrate racial separation, then the unifying power of rugby

✓ FIELD SIZE/Camera distance: For instance still no. 1 and 3, still no. 1 employs a medium shot with a reverse angle shot; still no. 3 (Matt Damon as Pienaar) is a close-up to focus on the expression of the face.

✓ Blurred/out of focus: When Mandela enters the rugby field, here the viewer's attention is focused on Mandela's importance; he is dressed in the Springbok jersey and ready to reconcile South African society.

✓ Voice-over: Clint Eastwood's movie title comes from the poem by William Ernest Henley, which is what Morgan Freeman is quoting from on the trailer's voice-over. "Invictus" is Latin for "unconquered".

Music:

✓ The first 20 seconds: the trailer opens with a classical string quartet that is melancholic as it deals with the last days of Mandela's imprisonment (Robben Island is shown at the beginning of the trailer)

✓ The central theme is led on a trumpet

✓ Then, with Mandela's inauguration, the music changes, tension is built

✓ In the second half (1:18) of the trailer the music changes with the recruiting of the captain to unite South Africa: The song is a traditional Xhosa hymn entitled "Hamba nathi Mkhululi wethu" which, roughly translated, means "Go with Us, our Saviour", supported by the acapella choir "Overtone"
→ Meant to echo the film's idea of coming together

M6 How Apartheid Died on a Rugby Field

John Carlin

1. Sum up the main events that are mentioned in the text. SB p. 62

- The text opens with the arrival of Mandela at Ellis Park.
- Then, the author uses a flashback and explains how the song "Shosholoza" was chosen to be the anthem of the 1995 Rugby World Cup: Dan Moyane, one of the rugby broadcasters during the World Cup, is asked by his co-broadcaster (John Robbie) about how to interpret the tone of song.
- Moyane therefore performs the song first on air, which attracts a lot of interest and approval by the audience.
- Next, Moyane presents the song on the rugby field to the fans, in order to show them how the words are pronounced and how the song is sung.
- As the fans are all participating and singing the folk song, an overwhelming atmosphere is created.

- Finally, Mandela, dressed in the jersey of the Springboks, enters the field at Ellis Park and is excitedly cheered for by all fans.

2. Examine by which means the author is convincing the reader that the Rugby World Cup was a unifying force for the people in South Africa.

John Carlin makes use of different means to convince the reader.

- Structure:
  The author starts his article as if it was a diary entry or journal, where he sums up the events in an enumeration (cf. ll. 1–4). Then he employs a flashback in which he elaborates on the background of the events before Mandela is welcomed by a thundering roar at Ellis Park (cf. ll. 5–18; ll. 19–55).
  At first glance, it seems that Carlin is simply re-telling the events but in between his accounts of the past events, he inserts comments that evaluate them ("[...] their blend of easy banter and serious political discussion was one of the more palpable contributions that emerged from civil society to help precipitate South Africa's political changes", ll. 11–13).
- Stylistic devices:
  anaphora in l. 7 "They needed [...]. They needed [...]",
  ➔ To understand the song the white fans needed support by black South Africans; the repetition of the words "needed" emphasises the recurring symbol of needing each other.
  enumeration in ll. 47–48 "a black street song, a soccer song, a migrant worker's song, a prisoner's song."
  ➔ To stress the origin of the song that is now used as one of the national anthems.
  alliteration in l. 59 "a moment of magic, a moment of wonder"
  ➔ To increase intensity and to re-emphasise the unifying power of rugby.
  direct quotes of contemporary witnesses like Dan Moyane and Morné du Plessis
  ➔ Direct quotes contribute to make the article more emotional
  analogy: first, Dan Moyane is the "naïve interrogator" (l. 20) and Jon Robbie the expert during the World Cup broadcasting. However, when it comes to the song "Shosholoza" Dan's role is reversed and he is the expert, which even leads to the performance on the rugby field at Ellis Park
  ➔ One can see Dan Moyane's change of role as he is the one who helps all fans, including white fans, to sing a unifying song.
- Style and tone:
  John Carlin predominantly employs emotional and vivid expressions: for example in l. 11 "blend of easy banter"; ll. 57–58, "the rugby man's eyes filled with tears"; l. 61 "mind-boggling".
  The tone of the article is positive, even euphoric and full of claims that leave no doubts that Mandela united South Africa with the power of sports: "And there it was. 'Nelson! Nelson! Nelson!' Fear melting away." (ll. 76–77); "the sea-change that Mandela had effected" (l. 72).

3. Compare the text at hand with Zapiro's cartoon that was published in the newspaper *Sowetan* in January 1996.

In the cartoon, Mandela is shown as a paper-doll figure, with different jerseys for rugby, cricket and football. Interestingly Mandela is always in position to greet and smile.

Some students might also think of a jumping-jack puppet.

The cartoon is far more critical, even sarcastic, compared to John Carlin's article who, as stated above, is inspired and thrilled by Mandela's actions.

4. Put yourself in the shoes of John Carlin and write a letter to the editor of the *Sowetan* in which you comment on Zapiro's cartoon.

Individual answers;
Content-wise, the letter should include:
- Carlin is not as critical as Zapiro who sees Mandela and his means of using sports to unify South Africa as sth. interchangeable.
- For Carlin, Mandela is a hero and not someone that can be mocked.

Form-wise, the letter should include:
- Salutation of "Sir or Madam" and introduction of yourself and your position
- Statement of the purpose of the letter, the article's headline/author, date of publication, as well as the initial reaction to the cartoon
- Explanation of your opinion (argumentative part)
- References to arguments mentioned in the article

M7 Dog Eat Dog

Niq Mhlongo

1. Have a look at the cover of the novel *Dog Eat Dog* and make an educated guess what this novel and the main protagonist's story might be about.
SB p. 64
Lying on a pile of books, a young man seems to be quite relaxed. His position on the pile might lead to assumptions that he is not interested in the books and, thus, in the education that is offered to him.

2. Point out Dingz's situation and his reaction to the letter of regret.
First, Dingz's (the protagonist's) application for financial aid is rejected from the University Bursary Committee again, so Dingz's reaction is to reflect about his life in the township where his family and he live in poverty with no property of their own. Dingz lives in the township of Soweto with no facilities, no job and not enough food. Dingz's initial reaction is to go to the Financial Aid Office: he ignores the queue and storms to the secretary. Although the secretary tries to stop him with harsh comments and by pointing at the queue and the signs, Dingz starts complaining aggressively and using racist vocabulary against the black secretary, calling her a bimbo.

3. Examine how far this excerpt is characterizing post-apartheid transition, focusing on diction.
Characteristics of post-apartheid transition:
- Dingz can study at the University of Witwatersrand.
- However, the main character does not have enough money to study or to keep up university life.
- Compares the hardships of living in the township to Dingz's university life.
- The fear of being thrown out of school, forced back to the daily challenges of uneventful township life (cf. ll. 54–65).
- Inequality caused by an apartheid that still lingers on (cf. ll. 35–39).
- Dingz's use of the term "bimbo" (l. 85) illustrates that the deep racial memories of apartheid still exist.

Diction (use of language):
- Stylistic devices: comparison in ll. 33–34, "a man who chops off the breasts of the mother as the hungry baby tries to suck fresh milk from them"; a metaphor in l. 32 ("cheese life") for good life.

→ This illustrates to the reader the implications that the letter of regret will have on Dingz's life
- Use of different styles: "izifebe" (prostitute in Is'camtho= urban language variety) to describe the township context.

- Dingz lives in two spaces:
  a) Life at university in 1994 (l. 49, "I was happy at the Y"; l. 54, "At the Y I could differentiate between my meals").
  b) Life in the township before 1994 and in 1994 ("There was nothing exciting for me about living the life of the unemployed and unemployable, whose days in the township fold without hope.", ll. 39–40; ll. 46–48 "At home I still slept in the dining-sitting room. [...] I was woken up at four o'clock in the morning by the footsteps of my two brothers [...] before they went to work.").

➔ Portrays the contrast between township life and city life, whereas the latter offers opportunities, according to Dingz.

4. Discuss Dingz's behaviour in the bursary office against the backdrop of 1994 and his family situation.

Individual answers; the historical backdrop makes this novel so interesting: it is 1994, Mandela has been released from prison and South Africa is having its first free elections.

Of course the consequences of apartheid still exist and some students might argue that Dingz is simply fighting for what he has been dispensed for so long and that now the financial aid he urgently needs is denied, although his family lives in grinding poverty.

To spice up the discussion a quote by Niq Mhlongo might be helpful:

"the season of change when everyone was trying to disown apartheid."

M 8 South Africa's Police: Friend or Foe?

M 8a South Africa Tries to Take the Force out of Police

Steven A. Holmes

SB p. 66

1. Sum up the restructuring of the police and the problems still prevailing in 1994.

Restructuring of police:

- Symbolic change, they were renamed the South African Police Service (before: South African Police)
- A process of demilitarisation begins
- Command structures are changed and the provinces are given the power
- The new racial make-up represents the mixed-race population
- Political parties are consulted for the renovation
- A new bill is implemented that limits unjustifiable police operations (Bill of Human Rights)
- The communities decide where to place police stations
- New titles are assigned to police officers to signal the end of paramilitary hierarchies
- Police officers are trained in crime fighting and diversity workshops

Problems that still prevail:

- High crime rate; in 1993, 17,467 killings in a country with a population of 40 million
- Turf wars about drug trafficking between gangs in townships take their tolls and illustrate that nothing has changed in the townships
- Police try to intervene, again without warrants but neither the community nor the gangs are impressed
- Police operation in the townships leads rather to strong doubts than new trust

2. **Do some research on the history of police in South Africa. Prepare a presentation focusing on *South African Police* during apartheid, *South African Police Service* from 1994 onwards and the *Marikana Inquiry*.**

South African Police (during apartheid):

- First, only police forces for the Cape Colony, the Natal Colony, the Orange River Colony and the Transvaal existed; then they were formed into South African Police (SAP) in 1913 which were responsible for cities and areas around cities.
- In rural areas the South African Mounted Riflemen were policing.
- In the next 40 years the SAP started taking over the responsibilities of the Riflemen (1918), the South West African Police (1939) and, in 1986, the Railway Police Force.
- The SAP and army collaborated since World War II and in 1948 the relationship between police and army was strengthened.
- In 1958 (Police Act Number 7) the SAP had more functions and power, such as to prevent and stop unrest, especially from anti-apartheid activists.
- In 1965 the Police Amendment Act allowed police operations without warrant within a mile of any national border.
- A deeply racist organisation that played a crucial role in enforcing apartheid with violence and fear.

South African Police Service: see above;

The homepage of South African Police Service provides a historical sketch from 1994 onwards:

"Prior to 1995, South Africa was divided into the so-called TBVC States, Self-Governing Territories and Development Regions (old South Africa). The TBVC States had independent status but were not widely recognized by the international community. The TBVC States and Self-Governing Territories were also referred to as Homelands. TBVC States: Transkei, Bophuthatswana, Venda and Ciskei

Self-Governing Territories: Gazankulu, Kangwane, Kwandebele, Kwazulu, Lebowa and Qwaqwa

Every Homeland had its own policing agency, bringing the total number of policing agencies in the country to eleven (ten homelands and the old South African Police). All eleven policing agencies had different uniforms, rank structures and conditions of service and were established under different legislation.

With the adoption of the interim Constitution in 1994, the Homelands and old development regions were abolished and integrated into a united South Africa with nine provinces. The new Constitution established a single National Police Service for South Africa under the executive command and control of a National Commissioner who is appointed by the President.

On 29 January 1995, General George Fivaz was appointed by President Nelson Mandela as the first National Commissioner of the new South African Police Service [...]. National Commissioner George Fivaz had the responsibility to first and foremost amalgamate the eleven policing agencies into a single united South African Police Service and secondly to align the new Police Service to new legislation and the process of transformation in South Africa. [...]"

South African Police Service, "History", www.saps.gov.za [23.01.2015]

Marikana Inquiry:

On 17 August 2012, striking platinum miners were killed by a member of the police force. It is assumed that the police officers, heavily armed, were shooting into the crowd of 300 men.

Two days before, South Africa's deputy president Ramaphosa, who was then a shareholder of the Lonmin platinum mines, called the police to quell the unrest of the protesters by disarming and dispersing them.

The Marikana Inquiry Commission was appointed, arising out of the tragic events.

→ The police force is meant to enforce safety and morals but failed here again.

M 8b SAPS image

Zapiro aka Jonathan Shapiro

SB p. 68

1. Describe the cartoon.

The cartoon shows two police men dressed in uniforms. They are seen from the back, heavily armed with rifles. One of them is shouldering his rifle and the other one has his finger on the trigger. The officer on the left has a target on his back and the right man is targeted, as one can see a digital bullseye centred on his head. Together they are patrolling through a township, because on the left you can see shacks.
The black policeman says: "I'd say we're still suffering a bit of an image problem".

2. Analyse the cartoon – what is Zapiro criticizing?

During apartheid South African Police was a military-style organization led by white South Africans, which played a crucial role in maintaining apartheid with control and violence. The cartoon illustrates that the South African Police Service might have been restructured but people still do not trust the police despite the new racial makeup.
All in all, the cartoon points at the prevailing problems caused by apartheid.

3. Against the backdrop of what you have learned so far, discuss if the police in South Africa is a friend or foe.

<u>Foe:</u>
The South African Police played a crucial role during apartheid as it was a deeply racist organisation. Here it makes sense to refer to the sad events in the history of South Africa.
First, in the Sharpeville Massacre on March 1960, police officers opened fire on a large group of anti-apartheid protesters outside of the local police station, killing 69 demonstrators and injuring more than 150 people. A second example is the Soweto uprising during which the police began to shoot directly at the protesting children.
Furthermore, intimidating anti-apartheid activists and showing brutal performances in the 70s and 80s led to hostility between the police and the black population.
The shooting of 34 striking miners (August 2012) is another example of South African policemen turning towards violence.
To sum it up, in 1994 the police force might have been restructured, but nevertheless policing culture is something that had been developed during apartheid and is difficult to change quickly. As a result the police is confronted with a legitimacy crisis.
<u>Friend:</u>
In 1994 the South African Police was going through an extensive transformation process; two decades later the South African Police Service looks significantly different in its organisational culture and political culture.
For instance, damaged race relations were addressed with training (diversity workshops) and affirmative action policies were implemented.

M 9 Beyond the Figurehead

Itumeleng Mahabane

SB p. 70

1. Outline Mahabane's main arguments and state his criticism.

<u>Main arguments and criticism:</u>

- False sense of reconciliation between blacks and whites is created: blacks are asked to forget the past and whites are not responsible for the past; pre-1994 is ignored and deleted.

- The author doubts reconciliation with the development of sympathy and empathy but is convinced that the focus on common interests, like the economy, is working.
- Some reasons for this development is the African National Congress (ANC) and celebrating Mandela larger than life. This leads to two problems:
  - First, Mandela received lots of sympathy but blacks have to accept that Mandela received sympathy for their own sakes.
  - Second, no real criticism against Mandela or the assessment of his legacy is possible.
- All in all, mutual understanding is missing, which prevents society from real reconciliation.

2. **Analyse Mahabane's attitude towards Mandela. Focus on his presentation of facts and use of language.**

Attitude towards Mandela:

The author has a critical attitude towards Mandela's role and function after apartheid and demands a critical evaluation of Mandela's legacy in order to start a more genuine and authentic reconciliation.

Presentation of facts:

- Mahabane quotes many experts and pundits to emphasise that his article is presenting facts; for instance, Fulbright Professor Ann L. Phillips who defines different thresholds of reconciliation (cf. ll. 16–20) or economic consultant Duma Gqubule (cf. ll. 8–11).
- Mahabane quotes journalists who supported creating Mandela's legacy as gospel and did not allow the bereaved to mourn if Mandela was able to forgive (ll. 37–43).
- Mahabane indeed does not present any facts and figures (cf. Reconciliation Barometer) but states opinions.

Use of language:

- Embeds many quotes to make his article the voice of experts and journalists, for example ll. 9–10; ll. 12–14.
- Use of sarcasm: l. 1 "It was bound to happen and, thankfully, it has; ll. 1–2 "the sanctity of former president Nelson Mandela"; ll. 45–46 "the past can be relegated to the dustbin of history and thereby [...] absolve white of any responsibility [...]."; l. 40 "in the new moral lexicon of South Africa".
- Emotionally charged and eloquent language but not stilted: ll. 6–7 "the Mandela years safely locked in the hallowed hall, beyond questions"; ll. 37–38 "the most arrogant perhaps was a question posed in *The Star*".
- Use of rhetorical devices:
  - Parallelism: ll. 71–73 "the silence many blacks believe they were forced to endure [...] and the silence some whites feel they are expected to adopt now".
  - Contrasts: "past and present" and "black and white": ll. 54–56; ll. 71–73.

3. **Comment on the claim that Mandela was "creating a false sense of reconciliation." (ll. 9/10)**

Individual answers;

On the one hand, in 1994 South Africa was at the brink of a civil war and Mandela's pragmatic reconciliation served as a means to end the fear and risk of a civil war and maybe was, for that period, the right way to reconcile South Africans.

On the other hand, it is time to evaluate the policies Mandela initiated and triggered, which does not necessarily mean that this period of South Africa is not valuable or important but that debate is important and crucial in a democracy.

South Africa Education Crisis Fuels State School Exodus

Karen Allen

The article at hand was published in March 2012. The author investigates the education crisis and why some parents in Eastern Cape Province are opting to send their children to private schools despite the cost.

1. **Sum up** the present schooling situation as described in the article.

2. **Analyse** how far the text "South Africa Education Crisis Fuels State School Exodus" and the cartoon by Zapiro complement each other. Focus on content and language.

3. Write a letter to the editor in which you **comment** on the present schooling situation, including your results from the analysis.

flashy *auffällig, glitzernd*
subdued *gedämpft*
to replicate to copy
deprived disadvantaged
indictment *Armutszeugnis*

"We are not a flashy* family – I'm just an ordinary kid," says Simanye Zondani, 17, as he pores over his maths homework in the subdued* light of his home.
Since his parents died, his aunt has given up her smart "bachelorette" flat in Queenstown and opted instead for a house in the township.
It means she can now just about afford the £700 ($1,100) to send her nephew to private school.
Five thousand children, most of them from black families on modest incomes, are switching to independent schools annually.
The quality varies, but in Gauteng province alone, South Africa's economic hub, more than 100 new schools have applied for registration in the past year.
It is a response to a sense of failure in the state sector, argues Peter Bosman, the principal of Getahead High School, the low-cost private school which Simanye attends.
"Parents want consistency and quality," he says – not with a sense of schadenfreude but resignation. [...]
The irony is that significant numbers of parents who send their children to private schools are themselves teachers in the state sector.
For the past few years, the school has achieved pass rates of 83 % – 100 % for the secondary school-leaving certificate known as matric.
It is an impressive figure and is replicated* among other low-cost private schools in deprived* areas.
Nationally, fewer than half of all school leavers pass that exam – an indictment* of an education system that is dysfunctional, critics say.
Far from being well-endowed with land and smart buildings, Getahead High is situated in a disused warehouse.
It offers computers and sports facilities, which the vast majority of children who attend state schools can only dream of. But the principal insists it is not about bricks and mortar, but the quality of teachers.
Many of the staff have returned from retirement to teach at the school and earn 10 % less than their counterparts in the state sector.
About 30km (18 miles) down the road, a rural state school, Nonkqubela Secondary, is struggling with outdoor pit latrines which have fallen into disrepair, while a third of all teaching posts remain vacant.
"We used to have good results, but we are short of maths teachers, science teachers and when staff look at our facilities they decide not to come here," head teacher Khumzi Madikane laments.

He says he cannot blame parents who can afford it, migrating to the private sector. But most of his pupils are dirt poor*.

dirt poor very poor

Education in the Eastern Cape is in crisis, and the central government has taken over the running of the department after allegations of corruption and mismanagement. [...]

But the Eastern Cape is not alone. The growth of low-cost primary schools, in response to a lack of faith in the state sector, is a trend that is spreading across the country. The independent sector has grown by 75 % in the past decade.

"It's been driven by parent demand," argues Ann Bernstein from the Johannesburg-based think tank*, Centre for Development and Enterprise.

think tank *Expertenkommission*

The crisis no longer a dirty little secret, with the government itself admitting that 80 % of state schools are failing.

In a recent speech, Basic Education Minister Angie Motsheka revealed that 1,700 schools are still without a water supply and 15,000 schools are without libraries.

Last week, campaign group Equal Education launched a court case to force the government to provide equal infrastructure at all schools.

Ms Motsheka has already promised reforms and investment in infrastructure, but it is a Herculean task.

It also requires political courage, argues Ms Bernstein.

"We have research from various communities, and increasingly from government, saying that in many places, teachers are not in school on Mondays or Fridays, that many teachers have other jobs simultaneously and the actual amount of teaching going on in the classrooms is a fraction of what it should be," she says.

Political courage, it would seem, means tackling the unions*.

union trade union, *Gewerkschaft*

[...] But more than 17 years after the end of white minority rule, observers argue that South Africa is struggling with more recent phenomena: poor teacher training, corruption and maladministration, a highly unionised teaching profession and low morale.

Back in the township, opting for a private school has come with huge sacrifices for Simanye's aunt, Nokwezi.

"I've really had to squeeze myself but it is worth it – in state schools, if they have a disagreement the teachers go on strike," she says.

The surge of low-cost private schools shows no sign of slowing down. Thousands of other grandmothers, brothers and sisters are scraping together the funds to send a child to school.

Yet the vast majority of South African children have little choice but to opt for the local state school.

Despite the best efforts of some committed staff, the exodus from state schools could see a generation of underachievers left behind.

Karen Allen, "South Africa education crisis fuels state school exodus", www.bbc.com, 12.03.2012 [23.01.2015]

"Textbook distribution saga continues around lies and excuses"

1. Sum up the present schooling situation as described in the article and in the cartoon.

Text: The present situation in education is, according to Karen Allen, in poor quality. First, many families use all their savings and money to make sure that they can send their children to private schools as they have higher rates of passing the matric because of qualified teachers. There are also are well-equipped and offer appropriate facilities in comparison to their public counterparts.

Therefore more and more low-cost public schools are evolving due to the lack of constant and proper education in state schools, but still many students who cannot afford public schools are left behind.

Cartoon: The cartoonist, Zapiro, takes up the Limpopo textbook scandal, when schools in the Limpopo province were not provided with the textbooks the government or Basic Board of Education was supposed to deliver in January 2012, and they missed two further important delivery deadlines.

One can see a lorry inscribed with "Excuses and lies" on its right side. On the other side, children are running cheerfully out of a school building named "Limpopo".

The lorry, full of boxes, is unloaded by a worker who utters "No textbooks, just the usual load" and one can see the number plate that says "Dept. of Ed." The driver of the lorry is an unhappy looking woman, the Minister of Board of Education, Angie Motshekga.

2. Analyse how far the text "South Africa Education Crisis Fuels State School Exodus" and the cartoon by Zapiro complement each other. Focus on content and language.

Text: The text deals with the crisis in education and investigates on causes and reasons. Furthermore, the author includes political issues like the role of the trade unions in state schools (cf. ll. 53–61) and the sacrifices that families made to provide their children with good education. Also, the consequences of the lack of quality education are pointed at in the last sentence of the article (ll. 71/72).

Language-wise the BBC article focuses on the crisis of South African education as an impossible "Herculean task" (l. 52) and on the situation of the people concerned who are "dirt poor" (l. 37) and "scraping together the funds" (l. 67) ➔ emotionally charged and dramatic language.

Cartoon: The cartoon deals with the textbook scandal as a symbol of maladministration and crisis in education; it does not elaborate on causes or reasons but obviously blames the Department of Education and the minister, as "EXCUSES AND LIES" is written in capital letters on the lorry and the driver, the main force of the crisis, is Angie Motshekga.

Language-wise the cartoonist is accusing the Board of Education of lying and offering bad excuses.

3. Write a letter to the editor in which you comment on the present schooling situation, including your knowledge about education during apartheid.

Individual answer; (cf. chapter 2, M 9)

M1 Wrapped Up

Malika Ndlovu

1. Sum up the poem "Wrapped up". SB p. 72

The poem "Wrapped up" portrays everyday life in South Africa and emphasises a culturally diverse South Africa. The first stanza of the poem starts with the speaker's discussion with friends about the characteristics of South Africans and the search for an explanation of what South Africa is like. The second stanza enumerates various gastronomic specialities of Indian and Afrikaans origin.
Then, in stanza 3 crime-ridden Hillbrow is mentioned and that it is not such a bad place. The speaker encounters Buddhists and Christians in the next stanza, followed by meeting a drunken woman. Stanzas 6–7 deal with the car that needs to be repaired at a petrol station and the misunderstanding that the group of youths is looking for marijuana. In the lines of stanza 8, the youths listen to diverse music: e.g., REM and the anthem "Nkosi sikelele". Finally, the poem ends with the speaker's claim that there is no need to fight, one just needs to accept that they are all blessed.

2. Examine the spirit of contemporary post-apartheid that is wrapped up in this poem by Malika Ndlovu. Focus on form and language.

Contemporary post-apartheid spirit:
The poem "Wrapped up" is a positive poem as it portrays a very diverse and enriched South Africa in terms of food, religion, language and music. The central sentences of the poem are "there's mos a space for every face" (l. 12) and "this pot-pourri means we've been blessed" (l. 34), which underlines the tolerance and celebrates South Africa despite prostitution and crime (cf. ll. 17–20).
The message is that there is no apartheid, it's time to celebrate the nation's diversity.

Focus on form:
- Rhyme: the first stanza has a rhyming couplet; the second stanza offers rhymes in lines 3 and 5; in the third stanza only lines 2 and 3 rhyme (l. 11 "place" and l. 12 "face"); in the last stanza *REM* and *Die Stem* rhyme, as well as "stressed" and "blessed" → celebration and acceptance towards all cultures.
- No use of full-stops, which shows that the transformation process has started and is going on.
- Negative aspects of South Africa are also prevalent but the attitude is positive: in stanza three, "Even Hillbrow's not a bad place/There's mos a space for every face" (ll. 11–12).
- The first stanza is very interesting: if you look at the last words of every line, they can be read as the message of the poem: "bra" "are" "the nation", "the situation".

Focus on language:
- The title already alludes that the poem is about the wrapped up new South African life.
- Malika Ndlovu communicates the contemporary post-apartheid spirit with her use of a variety of English, which is *Kaapse Taal* and *Kombuis*, also called the Kitchen Language → a linguistic variety that communicates the new identity. For example: l. 5 "boerewors" (Afrikaans farmstyle sausage), l. 8 "samoosas" (Indian snack), l. 6 "breyani" (baked beans in breadloaf).

3. **Compare the message of the photo with the message that is conveyed by "Wrapped up".**
Individual answers; the poem and the photo convey the same message: both stress the positive attitude of change after apartheid.

M2 The South African Reconciliation Barometer 2013

SB p. 74

1. **The Reconciliation Barometer has a new focus every year. According to the photos, what were the targets of the surveys in 2011 and 2012?**
   - 2011: Missing housing and land and hardships of townships
   - 2012: South African youth, the lack of proper education, and the consequences of apartheid

   → Targets social issues as differences in a society might stop national reconciliation

2. **Read the data and statistics first and then describe what they are dealing with.**
See model solution, **Worksheet 7**

3. **Analyse the table on p. 75 (bottom) and the figure on p. 76 (top) from the Barometer in 2013 and compare them with the perceptions since 1994 (table p. 75, top). Do you think the perceptions of progress are correct? The skills pages (pp. 110 ff.) might help you.**
Analysis of the table p. 75 (top): The table shows the response to the question to compare the country the citizens experience today with what it was in 1994 on a number of issues. In general, citizens are more likely to say that things have improved rather than worsened, but this is not the case with regards to employment, income equality and the economy in general.
Analysis of the table p. 75 (bottom): This table shows degrees of material inclusion and exclusion with the living standard measures: obviously there are very poor and uneducated people and rich and educated citizens, which might suggest that material exclusion is closely linked with less or low education. But as the table does not offer any information about distribution or race, it is inconclusive.
Analysis of the table p. 76 (top): The table with the perceptions demonstrates that South Africans believe that race relations are improving and class relations are worsening. The relationship between race and the Living Standard Measure (LSM) reveals that in the lowest four LSM categories there is a higher percentage of black South Africans than in any other race group.
35 % of black South Africans are in the lowest four LSM categories, 48 % are in the middle categories and 16 % are in the highest categories. The opposite trend can be revealed for white and Asian South Africans, as the majority of them are in the higher LSM groups (5 % are in the middle categories and 95 % in the top four categories).
→ Class inequality seems to be evident.

4. **Discuss if South Africa's society is a splintered society.**
Individual answer;
+ Perceptions of the first table show that citizens believe the situation is improving which does not support the statement that South Africa is a splintered society.
– Consequences of apartheid (for example excluding blacks from education) still exist and show a society that is splintered in terms of economic distribution and education.

M3 Mandela Dies with Rainbow Nation Dream Still Work in Progress

Mike Cohen, Franz Wild and Amogelang Mbatha

1. Go back to the Living Standard Measure by race (figure p. 75, bottom) and focus on education. What is striking?

SB p. 76

Especially the citizens in LSM 1–3 demonstrate that material exclusion comes along with low education.

South Africa spends a bigger share of its gross domestic product on education (6.6% in South Africa in 2012) but the distribution of education shows inequality: only one in ten blacks qualifies for university, for example.

2. "I benefited from apartheid" – this is how the t-shirts created by Leonard Shapiro and Roger Young are labelled in order to dismantle unequal education in South Africa. Put yourself into the shoes of South Africans and write down your spontaneous reaction to these shirts.

Individual answer;

Some South Africans found the t-shirts are helpful to start a discussion about white privileged education; some South Africans claim that apartheid is the past and that all South Africans are legally equal.

Hier könnte man Original-Zitate und Reaktionen aus Zeitungsartikeln und Blogs nehmen, um den Schülern die unterschiedlichen, z.T. schockierten, aber auch wütenden und rassistischen Kommentare vor Augen zu führen.

"The political satirist Zapiro said: 'It evoked many vindictive and nasty responses from white people. I think it scratched a wound that is still open. There are some white people who still don't quite understand how brutal a transition we could have had, and how brutal a transition other countries have had. [...] Every white person, no matter how committed to the anti-apartheid struggle, benefited from apartheid,' he said. 'Anything that shows some people are aware of how much we benefited would be good.'"

David Smith, "'I benefited from apartheid' T-shirt sparks South African race row", www.theguardian.com, 16.11.2012 [23.01.2015]

3. Examine how the authors are presenting South Africa's present situation. Consider structure and contrasts.

SB p. 77

South Africa's present situation:

Disparities in income of blacks and whites, where 8.7 per cent of the 53 million South Africans earn six times more than black citizens. This is due to poor education. Moreover, black South Africans do not have the same access to medical care and proper housing; the Black Empowerment Act (affirmative action) under former president Mbeki enhanced the development of a black middle class, nevertheless in 2013 South Africa was downgraded from A3 to Baa 1 which represents a worse credit worthiness for South Africa's economy.

Structure:

ll. 1–9: Introduction in which the authors refer to Mandela's inauguration and the beginnings of the Rainbow Nation

ll. 10–18: Present situation in South Africa

ll. 19–28: Example of P. Tsotetsi

ll. 29–61: A historical sketch of the presidents and the ANC's policies and programmes with regards to employment, education, income and health

ll. 62–65: Conclusion – with the case of P. Tsotetsi, the dream of the Rainbow Nation has not been achieved

Contrasts:

- The authors are making use of past and present: they are contrasting what Mandela wanted to achieve and how far the Rainbow Nation got (l. 5 "a rainbow nation at peace with itself and the world" v. l. 62 "dream of a 'rainbow nation' is far from complete").
- Contrasting the current economic situation of black and white South Africa.

4. **"I don't choose to benefit from apartheid. When I was able to vote against it – I did," says a white commentator to the t-shirts. Put yourself into the shoes of P. Tsotetsi and comment on this quote, using facts from the text.**

Individual answers; P. Tsotetsi might say that the consequences of apartheid, disparities in education and, thus, in the income level have led to the fact that he has to eke out a living.

Helpful indirect and direct quotes to support this are in the text in ll. 16–18 and ll. 19–22.

To start a fruitful discussion about the quote it might be helpful to make use of the "Matthew effect", a phenomenon where the rich get richer and the poor get poorer.

In education the Matthew effect describes how new readers acquire the skills to read: early success in acquiring reading skills usually leads to later successes in reading as the learner grows, while failing to learn to read before the third or fourth year of schooling may be indicative of lifelong problems in learning new skills.

The Matthew effect simply states a vicious circle: without proper education → no job or good job → no income or low income → fewer chances for your children to improve

Subsequently, even if someone voted against apartheid, there is still a chasm between black and white, especially in terms of economy and of education.

5. **Assess the appropriateness of the t-shirt.**

Individual answers;

Background: The idea of printing these shirts started with job vacancies at a supermarket that were targeted for black recruits, which only led to an outcry by many whites. Roger Young printed the t-shirts with the statement as a reaction.

The t-shirts are appropriate as they make citizens aware of inequalities that were caused by apartheid and that still persist in South Africa; they can be seen as a courageous gesture. These T-shirts also explain why laws like black empowerment acts still exist. Moreover, it is important to talk about responsibility and race.

@ SNG-40657-015

Zapiro hat einen Cartoon zu der Kontroverse veröffentlicht mit dem Titel „Whites who never benefitted from apartheid", zu sehen ist lediglich ein leerer Rahmen (s. Webcode). Als Gegenpol zu den t-shirts von Roger Young und Leonard Shapiro könnte dies zu angeregten Diskussionen führen.

SB p. 78

6. **According to the OECD, education is the key to a working economy and the skills available in the labour force influence how countries will fare in the global market. So workers with higher levels of education are needed. The photo shows a typical classroom in rural areas of Eastern Cape. Justify the title of the text "Rainbow Nation Dream Still Work in Progress" with reference to the photo below.**

The photo shows that schools in outskirts or rural areas, with a high number of black South Africans, are neither well-equipped nor well-situated. Good schools are not located in poor areas, so those wealthy enough send their children to private schools which prepare better for the final exams. Only four in ten pupils that start school stick it out to pass the matric, the school-leavers' exam, though the pass mark is as low as 30%. Just 12% achieve high enough marks to get into university. And only 11% get a mark of 40% or above in maths.

Only 71.2 % of children that should be in grade six are literate, but to understand education in South Africa we should not forget where it came from.

7. **Go back to Mandela's inauguration speech (M 3, pp. 54 ff.) and the way he sketched South Africa: evaluate if this has come true. Prepare a presentation showing the progress and failures so far.**

SB p. 79

Mandela's vision: "a constitutional, democratic, political order in which regardless of colour, gender, religion, political opinion or sexual orientation, the law will provide for the equal protection" (ll. 48–50); a government based on democracy (ll. 51–61); "building a better life of opportunity, freedom and prosperity" (l. 65); "we will tackle the widespread poverty" (l. 71).
Progress: Many more now have access to clean water and electricity. Between 1996 and 2010 the proportion living on less than $2 a day fell from 12 % to 5 %. The racist legislation of apartheid has been abolished. The new constitution is liberal and inspiring.
Failures: Yawning gap between rich and poor: the gini-coefficient which was 0.63 in 2009 underlines the inequality; the Marikana Massacre portrays an incompetent and dubious SAPS; the standard of teaching is low, thus many jobs go unfulfilled; the official unemployment rate is around 25 %.

M 4 Crime Capital of the World?

M 4a Man – Superman – Gunman

1. **How does this photo make you feel? Collect adjectives**

SB p. 79

Individual answer; shocked, appalled; the picture is impactful, controversial, dramatic

2. **Describe the cover and the way Pistorius is shown in the cover.**

- Mode of address: The Paralympic 'Blade Runner' looks straightforward with an icy glare.
- Image: Oscar Pistorius appears on the front cover, positioned in the middle of the full-length photo; bare-chested he has a toned body and is dressed only in running tights and his prosthetics; his palms are closed and look like fists, thus Pistorius looks as though he is about to defend himself.
- Main lines: The headline "Man Superman Gunman" accompanies the dramatic full-length picture of the athlete; in white text, the words "Man Superman Gunman" appear with the font size increasing with each word that follows.
- Language: There is a word pun in the main lines: first *man*, then *superman*, then he turns into a *gunman*. So, the word "man" is complemented in the end to "gunman".
- Layout: The colour scheme of the cover is in shades of grey; the upper part of the cover is in light grey, the more the reader pans the view the darker the shade of grey gets before it turns into a dark grey.
- Cover lines: The article is entitled "Oscar Pistorius and South Africa's Culture of Violence".

3. **Analyse how Pistorius is presented by focusing on layout (colour scheme, text connotation and text placement) and the chosen photo of him.**

Colour scheme and text connotation: On the cover Pistorius is presented as dark, sinister and someone who is hard to read as he is first a normal man who lost his legs as a child, later a superstar ("superman") triumphing over his disability and then a

gunman, shooting his girlfriend. Obviously, *Times* used photoshopping to make Pistorius and his eyes look sinister.
The article uses the Pistorius story – which gripped the world's attention for a number of weeks – as a jumping point to examining South Africa's culture of violence and the fact that the 'Blade Runner' killed his girlfriend because violence in South Africa is far too common.

4. **Discuss if and in what way this cover is impactful and controversial.**
Individual answer;
Many South Africans think that the *Times* article is highly inappropriate as Alex Perry is jumping to conclusions on a painful and sensitive case. Moreover, gun violence might be prevalent in Africa but to lump this all together against the backdrop of the Pistorius case is sth. that many South Africans consider to be too generalizing.

M 4b Pistorius and South Africa's Culture of Violence

Alex Perry

SB p. 81

1. **Do some research on the word *laager* in terms of history and South Africa.**
Laager:
- South African: *camp*; especially: *an encampment protected by a circle of wagons or armored vehicles*
- The word is South African in origin, and originally referred to a formation used by travelers whereby they would draw wagons into a circle and place cattle and horses on the inside to protect them from animals or bandits. Thus, the term is identified with Afrikaner history, namely the Great Trek in the 1830s.
- In South Africa white citizens are sometimes accused of having a laager mentality which exists as a physical and psychological barrier.

2. **Speculate why Pistorius' case could be an example of the culture of violence in South Africa.**
Individual answers;
Pistorius, who used his own gun that he stored under his pillow, killed his fiancée whom he allegedly mistakenly believed was an intruder. This can be seen as a metaphor for South Africa's problems such as a high crime rate, including violence against women.

3. **Sum up Perry's arguments and point out his conclusion.**
Arguments:
- The high crime rate in South Africa made Pistorius believe he had to defend himself from an intruder in his apartment (cf. ll. 18–22).
- Pistorius and his girlfriend serve as a parable for South Africa (cf. ll. 26–27; ll. 117–120).
- The gap between rich and poor leads to poverty-driven crimes (cf. ll. 44–50).
- The lack of trust in legislation and executive (the police and ANC government are corrupt) leaves South Africans all by themselves (cf. ll. 54–74).
- Perry also makes the connection between Afrikaans settlers behind barbed wire fighting off the natives 200 years ago and the gated communities like Silver Woods where Pistorius lived (cf. ll. 80–86).

Conclusion:
- Perry concludes that Pistorius shooting his girlfriend was a conclusion of South Africa's past and its persisting inequalities, including the failures of present government.

4. **Examine the way the author presents the case and tries to persuade the reader of his conclusion.**

Presentation of the case:
- First, Perry, the author, juxtaposes idyllic holiday images of the couple Pistorius-Steenkamp with the violence and crime of shantytowns.
- An unbalanced and one-sided report; it seems as if the report was based subjectively on the observations as the author never mentions or hardly quotes his sources.
- Perry puts the crime in the context of Pistorius's case → the ANC is corrupt and wastes money, the police are unable to protect people ("negotiated settlement" l. 58); depicts a crime-ridden society that is "unable to rely on the state" (l. 75) and thus is left alone to protect itself.
  → Raging crime and violence in South Africa used as a defence
- Inequality runs along racial lines (Cape Town centre v. Cape Flats).
- All in all, the article generalizes when the author uses the Pistorius trial as an allegory for South Africa.
- Use of negatively connoted words that evaluate the society: "racially splintered society (l. 19), "fragmented" (l. 106), "falling apart" (l. 106), "pervasive and prevalent", "pervasiveness" (ll. 20/24; l. 53).
- Vocabulary connoted with crime: "gun violence" (l. 24), "beatings and killings" (l. 78).

5. **This article has been criticized by many South Africans for being shoddy and generalized. Comment on van der Westhuizen's (journalist for *Mail & Guardian*) quote "*Time's* combinations of facts and images conjure Pistorius' defence: he has to fend for his home and 'his family' against the murderous black man 'out there'."**

Individual answer; students might use arguments Perry uses that, for instance, the black intruder is a product of the state that cannot ensure public safety and it is not meant as a racist argumentation as Pistorius never mentioned race in his affidavit, but according to the Reconciliation Barometer 2013 (M 2) inequality runs along racial lines.

6. **Discuss if the Pistorius case exposes the fragility of the nation's post-apartheid settlement.**

Individual answer;

Pistorius embodied a national metaphor: a previously disadvantaged young man overcomes his disability. South Africa was very proud of Pistorius, but then he killed his girlfriend and part of his defence was that he believed she was an intruder. So, the case of Pistorius is taken up and South Africa's history is simply flattened out. There are several reasons for this:

First, in 2012 the mismanagement of the system of education became public and second, the police shooting of Marikana offered links to South Africa's past and reminded of apartheid. Finally, President Zuma was accused of using public money for his private homestead, which led to further evocations of the past that even the government is corrupt.

7. **The online version of the article does not provide any statistics about crime in South Africa. Do some research on crime statistics in South Africa in general and Cape Town since 1994. Try to find out whether the facts the author states are right or not.**

SB p. 84

Helpful sites: see Webcode

SNG-40657-016 @

The facts about crime are correct.

Homicide: Since 1994 the murder rate has decreased by almost 54% in 2012. According to the date gathered by WHO this still ranks South Africa amongst the highest homicide rates in Africa.

M5 Fool's Gold

SB p. 84

1. **Make an educated guess what "positive discrimination" might be about. Can you think of examples in Germany?**
Individual answer; affirmative action or positive discrimination is a policy to foster and promote disadvantaged groups in a society that were discriminated against; in Germany there are quota systems for women and handicapped should be favoured.

2. **Point what *BEE* is about, also have a look at the terminology box on page 87.**
BEE (Black Economic Empowerment) is a programme to redress the inequalities of apartheid: government and companies try to assign jobs to disadvantaged groups (PDC) to represent the socio-demographic structure.

3. **Examine the author's attitude towards *BEE*. Consider headline, the presentation of facts and line of argumentation.**
Author's attitude: According to the author, the disadvantages outweigh the intended advantages of *BEE*, which can be seen in the article's title "Fool's Gold". Furthermore, the author criticizes that *BEE* leads to nepotism within a favoured black elite that is close to the ANC government (cf. ll. 7–11) and, additionally, ANC makes use of its state power to accelerate the selling of stakes and thus controls the racial makeup of companies with the implementation of acts and high fines (cf. ll. 33–38; ll. 74–75).
Presentation of facts: The author presents many figures and statistics to underline the negative side effects of BEE but rarely mentions his sources – besides one time where he quotes *Forbes* magazine and an expert from Rothschild.
Additionally, he offers a historical sketch of the background of *BEE* (cf. ll. 14–15; ll. 18–22), how it was implemented in South Africa and that only a few are benefiting a lot (cf. ll. 43–44).
Line of argumentation:

- Introduction: Starts with M. Ramphele, an opposition politician, who experienced the atrocities of apartheid as anti-apartheid activist and boyfriend Steve Biko was killed by the police (cf. ll. 1–3). ➔ To emphasise that she supports *BEE* and its concept but not the nepotism that favours only a few.
- M. Ramphele then claims that the gold company (Gold Field) agreed to government-nominated empowerment partners for its South Deep mine. However, the group confirms it was investigating its Black Economic Empowerment (BEE) transactions (cf. ll. 7–12). ➔ Contrasting information to show that *BEE* transactions lack transparency and to suggest that the ANC is exercising power to benefit from *BEE*.
- The Economist then gives a brief historical sketch of *BEE* transactions: for example the stake selling of an insurer to ANC-connected blacks and the fact that the ANC "uses state power to speed them up" (ll. 26–27, them = transactions). ➔ ANC exerts pressure with state power.
- However, this does not lead to a broad-based distribution within the economy but rather to an exclusive black elite that is getting richer and richer and unemployment rate is higher than 25 % among blacks (cf. ll. 43–49; ll. 50–53).
- An expensive bureaucracy is cultivated that does not foster competition but leaves jobs vacant and, most important, does not solve the problem of a lack of qualified workers.
- Finally, Lucy Holborn is quoted who claims that affirmative action does not make any sense without proper education and thus without qualified and skilled workers (cf. ll. 67–72).

- In his conclusion, the author sums up the dilemma that the ANC is in charge and "not about to lose power". It even raises surcharges for those whose workforce is not racially representative (cf. ll. 74–75) which is, according to the author, counter-productive.

4. **The gini-coefficient is described as an aggregation of the gaps between the people's incomes. If everyone in a group has the same income the coefficient is 0. If the income goes to one person and none to the rest, the coefficient is 1. In South Africa the gini-coefficient is among the highest of around 0.7. Evaluate if the advantages or disadvantages of *BEE* dominate in South Africa.** SB p. 85

Advantages:
- Gives equal access to PDCs within a society
- Compensates for past discrimination and systematic economic suppression

Disadvantages:
- Instead of qualifications and experience, now the applicants' race determines if they get the job.
- This might lead to brain drain: qualified people leave the country
- Less qualified applicants from PDCs might think they do not need to be qualified as they will be hired anyway
- Government should rather think about supporting rural areas and invest money into secondary and tertiary education

M 6 She Doesn't Speak

Marita van der Vyver

1. **Point out why Anouk is not speaking.** SB p. 88

Anouk experienced a traumatic incident: her father was killed in a residential robbery. As Anouk feels guilty for not being able to act, she does not speak anymore because it hurts her to talk about the incident.

2. **Analyse how Anouk is coming to terms with the violent incident in the past. Focus on language and stylistic devices.**

Language:
- Use of the first-person narrator (Anouk): makes the reader identify with Anouk and biases the reader → moreover, we get to know what Anouk thinks and feels as she does not speak and is mute.
- Beginning of the short story serves as information where Anouk listens to her mother (cf. ll. 1–11), then the reader is in the traumatic experience (cf. ll. 11–17).
- Sarcasm: "my mother speaks enough for both of us".

Stylistic devices:
- Leitmotif and metaphor of "walls": the wall that Anouk's father built to protect his family and the wall that Anouk built to protect herself from the pain and guilt (ll. 25–26 "a few months before, my husband had built a high wall around the property to protect us" and ll. 28–29 "no one has been able to tell me about what you should do when something is so difficult that you simply can't talk about it") and the wall of words that her mother builds around herself to protect herself from the pain.
- Comparisons: ll. 10 f. "like a tap that had been opened, the words would just pour from her" → comparing her mother to a tap; ll. 30 f. "Forcing the sounds out of my throat like dry vomit." → comparing words to vomit to illustrate how much pain it inflicts upon her .

- Rhetorical question: l. 18 "Do you see what I mean?" ➔ to underline that her mother likes to speak.
- Parallelism: ll. 55–56 "my eyes are filled with tears, my ears are filled with the familiar sounds of the street" ➔ illustrates that Anouk is overwhelmed.

3. **Justify why this short story should be included in an edition about identity in South African short stories.**
Individual answers; issues of identities are a source of conflict and suffering, therefore this short story serves as a good example: moreover, Anouk gets her voice back, is able to speak for herself and comes to grips with the trauma she and her family have experienced

4. **Put yourself in the shoes of Anouk and try to explain to Rebecca why you have been mute for such a long time and what triggered you to talk.**
Individual answer; language and style should fit to Anouk's diction.

M7 Orania

M7a Orania – The Documentary

Tobias Lindner

SB p. 91

1. **Have a look at the first scene from the film *Orania* and the map. What kind of place (city, suburb, etc.) would you expect to see and which aspects of South Africa are emphasised?**
The first still of *Orania* looks as if Orania was a small village, placed in an idyllic rural area in the Northern Cape Province; considering the map, it seems as if Orania was far off and remote.

2. **Skim through the provided stills from the film *Orania* and speculate about Orania and its people.**
Individual answers; obviously about Afrikaans culture and identity.

3. **Watch the trailer of *Orania* (www.orania-film.de) and point out why Orania was founded.**
Orania was founded to preserve Afrikaans culture and identity. Moreover, the citizens of Orania do not like the idea of being governed by non-Afrikaners.

4. **Analyse the function of the camera perspective and the fact that there is no commentator or off-voice.**
The camera perspective creates the feeling that the viewer is in the community and is talking to the people which constructs an inner perspective.
Usually a commentator or off-voice describes the significance of a scene or adjusts information but in *Orania* the citizens are foiling the intentions and purpose of Orania. All in all, the camera perspective and missing off-voice unmask the citizens of Orania.

M 7b Eine Stadt nur für Weiße

Jean-Pierre Kap

1. Sum up the main information and mediate in English. SB p. 92

- The article from the *Frankfurter Rundschau* starts with a quote by Neville Brown who prepares himself to go to Orania, a settlement in the North Cape province where only white Afrikaner live.
- Orania has about 700 inhabitants and belongs to a private company which sells shares only to Afrikaner who speak Afrikaans.
- All work is done by the citizens and no blacks are allowed to enter Orania, so it is a whites-only enclave.
- Although the concept of Orania reminds of apartheid the government is not interfering, maybe because they believe that model of settlement will begin to run out sooner or later, but the settlement wants to expand its community to more than 20,000 habitants.
- This plan might work out as Orania prospers: the cultivation and selling of nuts works well, Orania is a safe place patrolled by the citizens and with the implementation of its own currency.
- To black South Africans in the surrounding villages, the citizens of Orania are intolerant and racist as all whites during apartheid had been.

2. Against the backdrop that in December 2012 the Xhosa community *Mnyameni* started a cooperation agreement with Orania in order to take up the concept of Orania, discuss if Orania is acceptable as a place of cultural heritage or if Orania is unacceptable because of its link to the history of apartheid.

Individual answers;

- Orania is legally a private area and everyone is allowed to do what he/she wants to do as long as it is not against the law.
- Mandela wanted a united South Africa where race does not matter and Orania is spurning the idea of the Rainbow Nation and even if a Xhosa community follows the same idea, it displays that the Rainbow Nation is still not achieved.

M 8 Generation Born after Apartheid Sees Mandela's Fight as History

Marcus Mabry

1. What do you expect when you hear the term "Born Frees"? SB p. 93

Young people born after apartheid (1994).

2. Present the attitude the generation born after apartheid has towards language, history and politics.

Born-frees see Afrikaans as a relaxed language that is part of South Africa and have a positive attitude towards it, although Afrikaans is closely linked to the Soweto uprisings. Interestingly, young people's attitude towards history (apartheid) is that it is not the source for present-day problems like poverty and unemployment. It is rather something they leave behind themselves.

Similarly, they have a positive attitude towards their future but in contrast they do not trust government or politics.

3. Examine how Marcus Mabry is presenting the born-frees. Consider the structure and language of the article.

Structure:
ll. 1–5: introduction of the attitude of born-frees (Ms. Magubane) and introduction of the main thesis that young people are oblivious about the history of South Africa.
ll. 6–18: gives proof for the thesis: contrasting the quote by a born-free with the Soweto uprisings and Mandela's fight.
ll. 19–25: defines and characterizes the born-frees.
ll. 26–40: further enlarges on born-frees' attitudes towards history.
ll. 41–68: facts and figures and analysis from the Reconciliation Barometer and other experts, stating that born-frees have a more optimistic and positive attitude towards their future expectations.
ll. 69–78: states that the born-frees are uninformed and naïve, according to the Reconciliation Barometer.
ll. 79–85: conclusion and quote of Ms. Magubane again, where she states that Mandela would have loved to see the South Africa they are building now.

Language:
- The born-free woman is presented as "sitting in her comfortable suburban living room" (l. 1) and as unaware when "doing something unthinkable", namely "affectionately praising Afrikaans." (l. 3); "it is almost impossible for them to grasp what it was like to see him emerge from prison in 1990 and become president" (ll. 16–17) ➔ born-frees are relaxed, comfortable and oblivious of history and the meaning of Afrikaans during apartheid.
- Contrasts history and the born-frees' attitude: The Soweto uprisings "was a seminal moment" "But to Ms. Magubane, "At the end of the day, Afrikaans is just a language" (ll. 10–12) ➔ born-frees are ignorant and do not care.
- The author portrays the generation born after apartheid as optimistic but naïve and uninformed about the problems they will face (cf. ll. 64–70; 71–78).

4. Against the backdrop of what you have learned so far about Soweto in 1976 (cf. Chapter 2), discuss the statement that anyone of African descent, due to the condemnation of Blackness, should remain vigilant when it pertains to understanding the past and hopes for the future. Also consider the statistics on p. 94.

On the one hand, it is good to see a generation that is inspired by N. Mandela as they are open-minded and optimistic about their future. Furthermore, seeing Afrikaans as part of the South African culture and heritage emphasises how open-minded they are and that the born-frees are embracing the concept of the Rainbow Nation easily. They are not lacking appreciation.
On the other hand, knowing and understanding history allows an understanding of where we came from and is therefore part of our identity. It is ignorant of born-frees to ignore history as the consequences of apartheid are still prevalent.

SB p. 95

5. The American photographer Krisanne Johnson has documented Born Frees for many years now. Have a look at the slideshow with her photographs and speculate on the life of young South Africans.

Individual answers.

M 9 Harambe (work together)

Hip Hop Pantsula aka Jabulani Tsambo

SB p. 96

1. Describe the singer's thoughts on South Africa today.

The song *Harambe* describes that South Africa's youth is not political and has never experienced racism, restrictions or violence.

But the youth also appreciate the sacrifices made by the previous generation so that they can be free and emancipated.

2. Examine by which means Hip Hop Pantsula is showing the disconnection between the generations. Focus on language and stylistic devices he is making use of.

Focus on language:

The song can be separated into two parts:

The first part underlines the disconnection when it is stated that the speaker did not experience apartheid and violence during that period: "never been called kaffir" (l. 3), "10 cops charging through my front door" (l. 4), "tear gas" (l. 5), "rubber bullet" (l. 6), "holding guns in my palms" (l. 7) and the speaker did not participate in the Soweto uprisings and "carrying Hector Peterson" (l. 8); → clearly showing that apartheid is part of history for him.

The second part, nevertheless, illustrates that he/she appreciates what he/she can enjoy today:

The speaker is "self-employed" (l. 12), "educated" (l. 16) and "emancipated" (l. 17).

Stylistic devices:

Hip Hop Pantsula employs a number of anaphoras (ll. 4–8, "Can't imagine [...]/Can't say [...]"), parallelisms (ll. 13; 16; 17 "Because of you") and repetitions.

→ All in all, on the one hand the speaker enumerates atrocities that the previous generations experienced during apartheid and he/she cannot imagine. But, on the other hand, the speaker is aware of his/her freedom.

3. Imagine you are a music journalist and have the opportunity to interview Hip Hop Pantsula. Come up with at least five questions you would like to ask him and write an interview.

Individual answer

4. Go back to the poem "Wrapped up" on pages 72/73 and evaluate, against the backdrop of what you have learned so far, if that poem still presents young people in South Africa.

Against the backdrop of *Harambe* and the article "Generation Born after Apartheid", the poem "Wrapped up" still presents the attitude of young people.

M 10 The Price of South Africa's Spending

SB p. 97

1. State the author's message.

The author thinks that South Africa's ruling party and president Zuma are symbols of decline.

2. After reading the article, explain its title.

Note: the original title of the article is "South Africa: The Price of Zuma's Spending". The article refers to the fact that Zuma has spent tax payers' money for his private dwelling and that this is not the only symbol of the decline of the ANC and the government. However, the fact that criticism about Zuma's spending is possible shows that South Africa is on its way towards a healthy and working democracy.

3. **Examine how the author characterizes present-day politics. Which attitude does he express and how is it conveyed?**

Present-day politics of the ANC:

- The author is critical towards the ANC and states that the fact that results for the elections in May 2014 will be below 60% is a sign of a competitive democracy.
- The discussions about Zuma's dwelling in Nklandla are not as important as that the opposition wants to start an impeachment because Zuma used public money to improve and upgrade his homestead. Moreover, Zuma lied about this.
  ➔ Present-day government is corrupt but at least the opposition is working.
- Nevertheless, the author emphasises that there is democracy in South Africa because of the possibility of investigation (Nkandla report).

Presentation of facts and language:

- The article refers to figures by Ipsos, a global market research to give an outlook of the results of the elections on May 2014 (cf. ll. 3–7).
- A biased and critical attitude can be seen in the expected election results: "barring an electoral catastrophe" (l. 2); "unlikely to be a resounding victory" (ll. 3–4).
- Further striking adjectives that the author quotes to create the illusion that he is not biased: "'appalling' manner" (ll. 19–20); "abused" (l. 20)
- Use of if-clauses in his conclusion illustrates that it is not clear how the president will react to the Nkandla report (cf. ll. 29–32).

M 11a Pistorius Trial: Nation of Competing Realities

Andrew Harding

SB p. 99

1. **Outline the article's message and describe the cover of the *New Statesman*.**

Article's message: South Africa is a country of disparities and the case of Pistorius is an allegory for these disparities.

Description of the cover:

- Mode of address: eye-level, straightforward
- Main lines: The shadow of Pistorius – The case tearing South Africa apart
- Language: allegorical, lurid headline
- Colour scheme: use of shades of grey
- Image: Pistorius is almost gigantic compared to the background; he looks straightforward and very determined; he is positioned very much in the centre; interestingly his shadow (mentioned in the title) is relatively normal in size

2. **Compare in how far the cover of the *New Statesman* and the article below could be seen as complementing each other. Focus on the language used in the article and on the cover, also taking into account the image used.**

Language in the article:

The author believes that South Africa is a nation of competing realities: "nation of notorious inequality" (ll. 1–2), "sharp contrasts – in wealth" (ll. 3–4).

Furthermore, with the trial of Pistorius police have shown that they lack competence in dealing with the crime scene (cf. ll. 23–28), in contrast, part of Pistorius' defence team, who were once public officers, are the best pundits in South Africa ➔ illustrates the inequalities.

Language on the cover:

The contrasts shown here (black and white image, Pistorius' shadow, which is a shape produced by a body coming between rays of light and a surface) indicate that there is more behind the Pistorius trial.

→ The cover and article complement each other as both deal with the Pistorius trial, which serves as a parable for South Africa's problems: The cover shows a shadow and the text deals with the case as a trigger to talk about competing realities in South Africa since the trial gives a reality check on police, gun violence, violence against women, etc.

3. **Discuss if the title "The shadow of Pistorius. The case tearing South Africa apart," is appropriate.**
Cf. model solution, **Worksheet 8**

M 11b Rainbow Nation – Myth or Reality?

SB p. 101

1. **Take turns with your partner(s), describe the various pictures, data, etc.**
Individual answer; partners should take turns and make sure the conversation does not get stuck. The language support on pp. 113 f. (SB) might be helpful.

2. **Decide which two pictures are the most and the least convincing representation of the idea of the Rainbow Nation. Together, come to a conclusion if the concept of the Rainbow Nation is a myth or reality.**
Individual answers; partners must come to a conclusion.

Model Solution (M 2, SB p. 74)

2. Read the data and statistics first and then describe what they are dealing with.

The statistics and data present the results of the Reconciliation Barometer survey on questions of unity, division and material exclusion. Furthermore, it discusses the living standard measure (LSM) as a measure for material exclusion and examines the relationship between this variable and race.

The first table, "Perceptions of South Africa's progress since democracy", summarizes the response to the question which asks South Africans to compare the country they experience today with what it was in 1994 on a number of different issues.
In terms of race relations, 44 % of South Africans assert that these have improved and only 17.4 % think they have worsened. In terms of family life, hope for the future, moral values and personal safety, about 40 % of South Africans report that these aspects of social life have improved, and the figures for disagreement range from 21.3 % to 26 %.
Economic circumstances have rather improved (39.5 %) than worsened (24 %) according to the perceptions of the people questioned.
However, the first table shows that employment opportunities have worsened rather than improved: 42.1 % think their employment prospects deteriorated compared to 1994. Moreover, the gap between rich and poor has rather widened (36.7 %) than narrowed.

The second table shows the living standard measures (LSM) developed by the South African Audience Research Foundation (SAARF) and describes the dominant characteristics of each grouping.
South Africans with the lowest standard of living are subsumed under LSM 1–4. Respondents in these categories are likely to live in a traditional hut, shack, or matchbox house, with an average income of less than R 3,200 per month. They have little access to services such as electricity and water on a plot.
LSM 5–6 present the middle groups who live in improved matchbox houses or townhouses and have access to water and a flush toilet. Comparing social activities and durable goods such as TV sets and fridges, LSM 1–4 have minimal or no access to these activities and goods, however those belonging to the bracket LSM 5–6 are baking for pleasure, hire DVDs and have more goods.
LSM 7–10 represent those who live in urban areas and have a household income of more than R 8,700. They have access to all services, participate in all activities and have access to all media.

The last figure presents the relationship between living standard measure (LSM) and race. One notices that in the lowest four LSM categories there is a higher percentage of black South Africans: 35.4 % of black South Africans are in the lowest four LSM categories, 48.2 % are in the middle categories and 16.3 % are in the highest four categories. White and Asian South Africans are almost absent from the lower LSM groups whereas a high percentage can be found in the top four categories.

Model Solution (M 11a, SB p. 99)

3. **Discuss if the title "The shadow of Pistorius. The case tearing South Africa apart," is appropriate, against the backdrop of the given text and cover, and your knowledge gained about South Africa so far. Give specific examples to back up your arguments.**

The message of the *New Statesman* cover and of Andrew Harding's article are unambiguously pointing to the Pistorius trial as a national metaphor, exposing the nation's post-apartheid society

At first glance, it seems that the case of a man cannot tear South Africa apart, as Oscar Pistorius is not representing South Africa. But his defenders have used South Africa's high crime rate to explain and justify what led him to opening fire on his girlfriend who was locked in the bathroom. The affidavit given by the athlete, allegedly mistaking Reeva Steenkamp for an intruder, makes the Pistorius case a metaphor for South Africa's problems.

However, there are arguments against the idea of a South African parable. On the one hand, guns, fear of God and self-sufficiency are stereotypes that certainly do not apply to all Afrikaners and for that reason, Pistorius is not a mirror for contemporary South Africa. A criminal trial is about weighing specific and singular evidence: this is a court case, not a parable.

Moreover, Oscar Pistorius, a hypermasculine icon and the first athlete to compete in the Olympic Games with prosthetic limbs, was doomed to fail when he was fashioned by media as "Blade Runner" and a crossover hero. Blaming him now for all of South Africa's shortcomings and using the Pistorius trial as a parable is not fair.

It goes without saying that South Africa is a young democracy and still in a state of transition. Hence, it takes some time to undo all inequalities, as the vestiges of apartheid (1948 to 1994) still shape society and politics.

On the other hand, as stated in the beginning, high crime rates are used in Pistorius' defence to show that his alleged fear of an intruder was not uncommon. There are reports of robberies where people are attacked by armed gangs while they are in their houses. In 2013, for example, 49 households were attacked each day. Furthermore, the case deals with two demons of South African society: violence against women and murder. An analysis of interpersonal violence suggests that income levels matter and that murder rates are driven by poverty and social ills. This is also what the author of the article refers to when he states that South Africa is "a nation of notorious inequality", marked by "sharp contrasts" (ll. 1–4).

Experts say that with the Pistorius case a mirror is held up, putting South African justice on trial and with it the South African police. During apartheid the police played a crucial role by using violence and supporting segregation, so policing required major reforms which were implemented under Mandela. However, police bungling creates an unflattering picture of the judicial system and shows the ineptitude of the South African police (cf. ll. 26–31).

Another aspect that should be mentioned is the verdict: Judge Masipa, presiding judge in the trial of Oscar Pistorius, was a figure of pride for many South Africans, being one of the first black female judges, born in Soweto in 1947, one year before apartheid was implemented. In the dock stands a white-middle class man, but a black woman decides the defendant's fate, so there is almost an inversion of the social dynamics in High Court. But now this former pride is matched with disappointment, leading to disparagements of Judge Masipa's gender and race. This again reminds South Africans how elusive the Rainbow Nation still remains.

All in all, the *New Statesman* cover supports the main message of the text, is therefore appropriate and fits the BBC article because both deal with South Africa's "competing realities" (l. 49), as the cover and article take up the Pistorius trial as a parable for South Africa's political and social ills.

To put it in a nutshell, I come to the conclusion that the arguments in favour of the visual and the text outweigh the thesis that Pistorius murder trial and verdict are simply a court case, since both shed light on the country's high levels of crime and its judiciary. Together, they illustrate that the case and the reactions to it are tearing South Africa apart.

Skin Deep

In the following article, published in *The Economist* in March 2008, the author deals with racial integration in the Rainbow Nation.

1. **Sum up** the author's message.
2. **Analyse** the author's attitude towards racial coexistence in 2008. Focus on the presentation of facts.
3. **Discuss** if "the ideal of a rainbow nation is fading" (l. 14) and take the figures (below) into account.

RACE is again on South African front pages and in the airwaves. A video film made by four white university students depicted a mock initiation of five middle-aged black cleaners into their student residence, showing them on their knees eating food on which one of the students had apparently urinated. The film, intended to undermine racial integration in student residences, sent shockwaves throughout South Africa and beyond.

It comes on the heels of several other ugly racial incidents. In January an armed white teenager went on a rampage* in a rural settlement, killing four people, including a mother and her baby, apparently for racist motives. Last month Irvin Khoza, the black leader of the committee organising the football World Cup tournament in 2010, sparked angry reactions when he told a journalist to "stop thinking like a kaffir" – an offensive word for a black African. The Forum of Black Journalists, a press lobby, got into hot water for barring* white colleagues from attending a meeting with Jacob Zuma, the ruling African National Congress's new president.

Fourteen years after apartheid, is the ideal of a rainbow nation fading? Not at all. South Africa has come a long way since the days of institutional racism. Its transition to democracy has been remarkably smooth, set against the country's bitter past. You hear of few incidents of racially motivated violence. The vast majority of South Africans want a non-racial democracy that respects people's differences. There are laws to punish unfair discrimination, and "black economic empowerment" – a positive-discrimination policy – seeks to redress* past injustice.

Though the poor and unemployed remain disproportionately black, an emerging black middle class is slowly blurring racial and social lines. Once-segregated schools and universities now include students of all colours. Even at the formerly all-white University of the Free State, where the racist video was shot and where tuition* was once in Afrikaans (the language of the early Dutch settlers), most students are now black. A rising majority of South Africans think that race relations are improving.

Yet South Africa is far from colour-blind. People of different races often eat in the same restaurants – but at different tables. Peaceful coexistence, which South Africa generally enjoys, does not mean integration. People in rural areas are even less likely to mix than those in large cities such as Johannesburg.

According to David Maimela of the South African Students' Congress, formerly white universities have paid only lip service* to integration. The Freedom Front Plus (FF+), a small opposition party representing mainly Afrikaners, opposes what it calls "forced integration" of student residences and says that Afrikaners who fear their cultural identity and language are threatened are not being heard. But Tim du Plessis, editor of *Rapport*, a popular Afrikaans weekly, says that legitimate issues to do with language have been used as a pretext to resist racial integration.

Many white South Africans, both Afrikaans- and English-speaking, feel increasingly frustrated by affirmative action. Where Nelson Mandela inspired many of them with his national vision, his successors – including President Thabo Mbeki – have generally failed to

to go on a rampage to behave violently

to bar *jmd. ausschließen*

to redress to compensate for sth.

tuition here: teaching language

to pay lip service to sth. *ein Lippenbekenntnis ablegen*

to abhor to feel disgust for sth.

to upbraid sb. *rügen, zurechtweisen*

do so. Many whites think the ANC is losing the moral high ground, and are becoming more insular and withdrawn – or are just emigrating. At the same time, many of their black compatriots feel frustrated by the slow pace of change.

Yet most South Africans, whites included, genuinely abhor* crude racism. The student video has shocked almost everyone, and has been condemned outright across the racial and political board, including by Afrikaans organisations and the FF+. The measure of South Africa's success is not whether it manages to eliminate racism – no multiracial country in the world has done that – but how it deals with it. Protests against the video incident have been contained and violence largely avoided. The four students may face charges. Mr Khoza of the World Cup committee has been upbraided*. The South African Human Rights Commission is looking into complaints against the Forum of Black Journalists. Tseliso Thipanyane, the commission's head, says, "We should be actively engaging one another on issues of race, rather than wish it away."

Group intolerance is not just a black and white issue. A recent poll by TNS Research Surveys, a local outfit, finds that 42 % of people living in shacks, facing the fiercest competition for jobs and services, feel threatened by "other cultures", far more than the national average of 29 %. Attacks by black South Africans on Somali shopkeepers and hostility to Zimbabwean immigrants both appear to be rising. The housing shortage in the Western Cape adds to tension between Coloureds (mixed-race South Africans) and blacks. In a country as diverse as South Africa, all this is to be expected. The video incident has made everyone think harder about how to promote greater harmony.

"Skin-deep", www.economist.com, 06.03.2008 [26.01.2015]

Do South Africans believe that the country is moving in the right or wrong direction?

Since 2009, the number of South Africans who believe that the country is moving in the right direction has declined significantly, while the number believing it's moving in the wrong direction has increased.

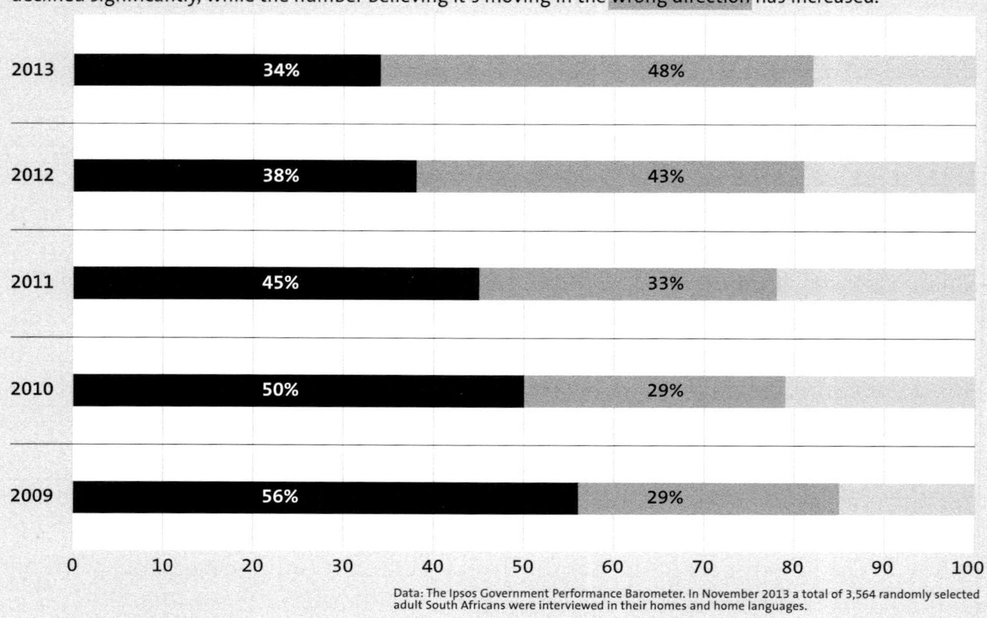

Mari Harris, "50 % of South Africans think Zuma not performing well – Ipsos", www.politicsweb.co.za, 12.02.2014 [22.01.2015]

1. **Sum up the author's message.**

First, the author is asking if the concept of a rainbow nation is weakening in South Africa and comes to the conclusion that it still prevailing but integration or racially-mixed groups hardly exist. Finally, he states that this is something society needs to work on.

2. **Analyse the author's attitude towards racial coexistence in 2008. Focus on presentation of facts and persuasive techniques.**

Attitude towards racial coexistence:

- The author is convinced that racial coexistence is still not working as many incidents prove the contrary (cf. ll. 1–13), but he underlines in several quotes that this is a challenge important to combat: "We should be actively engaging one another on issues of race" (ll. 52/53) and "[this] incident has made everyone think harder about how to promote greater harmony" (ll. 60/61)
- Moreover, he claims that racial disintegration is not simply an issue of black and white but rather connected to the economic situation of the people (cf. ll. 54–60).

Presentation of facts, e.g.:

- Opens the article with a video of racial incidents that is circulating and further episodes where people from different races exclude each other or treat each other in a derogatory way to illustrate that racial integration is not working yet, especially among young people.
- Quotes many sources like Freedom Front Plus (FF+) and the South African Human Rights Commission to present a well-founded and justified article.
- Is rather optimistic and believes that the Rainbow Nation, despite the existing problems South Africa has to face, needs to be worked on (cf. ll. 14–20).

Persuasive techniques, e.g.:

- Use of idioms: "it comes on heels of several ugly racial incidents" (l. 6)
- Repetition of key words: "peaceful coexistence" (l. 28); "integration" (l. 29); "racial and social lines" (l. 22) to emphasise the importance of cooperation
- A plea to underline his message: "the video incident has made everyone think harder about how to promote greater harmony" (ll. 60/61).

3. **Discuss if "the ideal of a rainbow nation is fading" (l. 14) and take the figures (below) into account.**

Individual answer;

On the one hand, the apartheid regime was voted out of office in 1994 and a modern constitution with freedom and all basic principles of elections and compulsory education was implemented. Moreover, the economy was strongly growing until the international financial crisis affected South Africa, for example Johannesburg is one of the world's financial centres.

On the other hand, political parties are still without any political agenda or programme. Administration is corrupt (Nkandla Report; Marikana Massacre, Limpopo textbooks) and disparities along racial lines are prevalent.